TATTING

TECHNIQUE & HISTORY

Elgiva Nicholls

DOVER PUBLICATIONS, INC.
New York

The cover design was tatted with 11 skeins
of DMC Size 5 Pearl cotton (Art. 115), color #738.

Published in Canada by General Publishing Company, Ltd., 30 Lesmill Road, Don Mills, Toronto, Ontario.
Published in the United Kingdom by Constable and Company, Ltd., 10 Orange Street, London WC2H 7EG.

This Dover edition, first published in 1984, is an unabridged and unaltered republication of *Tatting*, first published by Longacre Press Ltd, London, in a Vista Books edition in 1962.

Manufactured in the United States of America
Dover Publications, Inc., 31 East 2nd Street, Mineola, N.Y. 11501

Library of Congress Cataloging in Publication Data

Nicholls, Elgiva.
Tatting : technique and history.

Reprint. Originally published: London : Vista Books, 1962.
Bibliography: p.
Includes index.
1. Tatting. I. Title.
TT840.N558 1984 746.43'6 83-20602
ISBN 0-486-24612-4

Contents

List of Plates

Acknowledgements

Acknowledgements are made to those who have kindly lent old tatting books, from which the development of the craft has been compiled, and particularly to N. M. Lewis, an authority on old patterns, whose specialized knowledge and manual skill have also contributed to the text and illustrations.

The author is indebted to the DMC Library for information concerning the life and work of Thérèse de Dillmont.

FOREWORD TO PART I

THE object of the first part of the book is to give the reader a knowledge of tatting, first through its early beginnings and its development in the hands of those who brought it to the art it is today, and secondly through an understanding of its construction.

To those who do not know its possibilities, and especially its limitations, a piece of tatting does not mean very much. A superficial glance will tell if it is well worked; beauty is in the eye of the beholder, and either it pleases or it does not. But to understand it, it is necessary to be aware of more than this. A piece of tatting, from the simplest edging to a fabric the size of a shawl, is made of little pieces which, like the objects in a kaleidescope, can be arranged in innumerable positions: every designer finds new ways of placing them. The basic units are the ring and the chain: with these every design is composed (or of ring or chain exclusively), whether into well-known traditional formations or into more original groupings.

To recognize the formations and to appreciate the newer groupings is to understand them. If they are understood they can be described: if correctly described they can be copied. The first part of the book is devoted to what the ring and chain can do: how they have been, and can be, used: with this knowledge the observer can analyse and assess, even reproduce, any example which is put into her hands.

CHAPTER I

Definition of the Craft of Tatting

'A KIND of knotted work, used for trimming' and 'A kind of lace' are dictionary definitions. What then is lace and the properties which distinguish it from other fabrics produced from a spun thread?

'The chief characteristic of lace in all the stages of its development is its contrast to the uniform surface of woven fabrics. Lace is a combination of open spaces and compact texture, of transparent and opaque patterns, of light and heavy parts. In its most delicate form it has become a light, flimsy texture, the most subtle expression of textile art. . . . Its first appearance was in the sixteenth century.'

So writes an authority on lace structure; and tatting does in effect conform to this definition, in its essentials. It could in fact be termed 'poor man's lace', for at one time it was used as a representation of the fine laces worn at Court by aspirants to fashion. In 1851 at the Great International Exhibition, a certain Mlle Riego de la Branchardière received four awards including the Prize Medal for 'the skill displayed in the imitation of old Spanish and other costly laces'.

While real lace required a pillow, pins, a number of bobbins, needle and thread, a net foundation, etc., according to its kind, all that was needed for tatting was the hand, for the stitch is formed over the fingers: the shuttle merely carries the thread in a convenient manner, more convenient than a ball of some size. The stitch could also be formed by a needle on a long stretch of thread, or indeed without the aid of either. Tatting is in fact so simple that it is frequently confused by the uninitiated with crochet, which often appears to resemble it. The only feature it has in common with crochet (and knitting) is the fact that it is worked from one thread direct from the ball (or shuttle). Fabrics so made are distinct from those woven on a loom, in which one thread weaves in and out of warp threads previously set up on a frame.

In knitting, the stitches are supported on needles; in crochet the new stitch is hooked into the previous one; but in tatting each stitch is an independent progression, 'out of the air', relying neither on mechanical support nor upon previous stitches. Crochet is formed of intersecting loops, which stretch according to the nature of the thread used: the shape of the article is inclined to collapse when it is suspended. Tatting is a row of knots carried on a core of an internal thread: it is therefore firmer and stronger.

One of the features of lace is that it can show something of contemporary life and custom pictorially, by depicting through its design royal, heraldic or historical motifs, figures, etc. incorporated in its structure. In a more limited manner, the same can be said of tatting. In the free-style technique, stylised representations of flowers portraying the national emblems have been made, and older pieces for ecclesiastical use show biblical subjects. Carved stone tracery and lace are very closely allied; tatting also, as it is able to indicate architectural styles – gothic, rococo, flamboyant – in some degree. But apart from design, the uses to which tatting is put are a strong indication of the customs of the time. Lace was too delicate, too slow to make, to be used for common articles. Tatting could be in everybody's hands, as it could be made of very thick thread if required. It follows the fashion in dress and furnishings, and what are now called accessories. Trimmings on drawing-room aprons, cravats, antimacassars, covering for a parasol, were common in Victorian times: earlier there were lanyards to carry fans attached to the Regency waist belt. These were made of thick silk cord and required very large shuttles. Head-shawls, jabots and fichus were produced in the Netherlands: the most delicate and imaginative insertions and edgings came from the shuttles of France, where underclothes were so lavishly trimmed in the 'nineties, using the finest thread. Adornment for church vestments and altar cloths, in gold thread carrying precious stones, came from eastern Europe at a later period. Many of these articles, now no longer in common use, tell something of the history of the time. So do our contemporary patterns, reflecting the taste, skill, and requirements of today.

As a craft, tatting both gains and loses in working conditions over the years, rising and waning in popularity. The very fine earlier pieces must have been constructed by the light of a candle (perhaps refracted through a glass bowl of water, an old lace-maker's method of focusing the rays of light on to a single point). Now at least there is adequate artificial light. On the other hand there are a greater number of distractions, in the form of alternative and attractive types of hand-work, and the competition of television, with which it now has to contend.

Like many crafts, after a dormant period, tatting depended on someone sufficiently gifted to bring it again to popular notice, and to carry its evolution a step farther. During the last hundred years, four names are outstanding. But before this, and during the eighteenth century, very little seems to have been written, or at least preserved, on the subject at that time. It must have been a peak period, since constant reference is made to it in later works, by almost all the nineteenth-century writers, and the distinctive shuttles of that period remain as evidence. It was certainly a royal accomplishment in both England and France early in the eighteenth century and before. In England, William of Orange and Mary were on the throne from 1689 to 1702. In 1707 Sir Charles Sedley published a short poem called 'The Royal Knotter' referring to what is described by Lady Hoare as 'the Queen's homely habits'.

'Oh happy people! We must thrive
Whilst thus the Royal Pair doest strive
Both to advance your glory.
While he (by valour) conquers France
She manufactures does advance
And makes thread fringes for ye!

'Blessed we! who from such Queens are freed,
Who by vain superstition led,
Are always telling beads.
For here's a Queen now thanks to God!
Who when she rides in coach abroad
Is always knotting threads.'

This appears to be the first recorded reference to tatting in this country. (Mary was the daughter of James II by his first wife. As she married into the Dutch royal house, she presumably spent some time in Holland. Did she introduce it from that country, or was it already known in England?)

It has been said that the employment of the shuttle shows off the worker's hands to greater advantage than any other instrument of needlework. In 1759 Sir Joshua Reynolds painted the Countess of Albermarle with a shuttle in her hand. The portrait is in the National Gallery. In the following year Anne Chambers, Countess Temple, was painted by Allan Ramsay. The sitter, who is wearing a tight, long-waisted dress profusely trimmed with lace, holds a rather large jewelled shuttle; her piece of work, to which the shuttle thread is attached, is concealed in the lace-trimmed 'pocket', suspended by a ribbon from the left wrist.

Early books

So far as I have been able to discover, the earliest book on tatting that has survived is a little volume entitled *The Ladies' Handbook of Millinery, Dressmaking and Tatting*, published in 1843, one of a series of many handbooks on needlework and embroidery. This particular volume was described as the '2nd thousand' (impression) so presumably the first thousand was circulated either earlier in the same year, or before. In this second impression, reference is made to *The Ladies' Worktable Book*, whose first edition must therefore have been out before this. (The only edition available of the Worktable is the third, which was published in 1850.) In these separate books, the short section on tatting is the same – no progress is recorded in the interval. In the preface to the section, the writer states:

'This kind of ornament for children's and other dresses was once in high repute, and again appears likely to become a favourite. It certainly is very pretty, and can be laid on the bottom or edges of various articles of attire, in an almost infinite variety of forms. It is made by the hand: and the material employed is thread or cotton. The instrument used in making it is called a tatting needle [the engraving shows a shuttle] and can be procured at any of the fancy needlework establishments. The annexed engraving shows how the fingers are placed, while the loop is forming: and this, together with the following directions, will, we hope, enable our readers to execute, after a few trials, this very difficult kind of work.'

Not much of an encouragement to the beginner. Nothing could be simpler, and indeed less inspiring, than the three illustrated motifs – one can scarcely call them patterns – which give not so much as a glimpse of the nature of the 'infinite variety of forms' as promised.

'Tatting open stitch' shows two adjacent partially drawn-up rings, which are called scallops, with quite long loops (picots). 'Star Tatting' shows three rings (each of six long picots) arranged to form a triangle, but with no joins indicated. 'Common Tatting Edging' shows a row of small partially drawn rings, each of twenty stitches. The directions are extremely scanty.

The early 'forties must have been a period when the craft was suffering a severe depression. Its contemplated revival could not have received much stimulation from the collection now offered.

But a real awakening was not far away. The advent of the next decade saw what almost amounted to a rebirth of the craft in the hands of a practical and skilful pioneer, who amalgamated British and French talent.

Mlle Eleonore Riego de la Branchardière

Born in England, the daughter of an Irish mother and a French nobleman escaped from the Revolution, this remarkable woman (Riego for short) devoted her life to the invention and practice of many types of needlework and embroidery, on which she wrote over a hundred books between 1846 and 1887. The needle and shuttle carried her to fame and distinction. She was by appointment 'Artiste in needlework' to the Princess of Wales, working for and teaching the royal families of England and Germany. She claims to have introduced tatting from France, but this we have seen is a misapprehension.

She wrote eleven books on tatting, from her London residences. Her developments through the years show the principal evolutionary steps which carried it by 1868 – (the date of her last publication) almost to the point it is today – construction has altered little since.

Construction comes before design: only when methods have been evolved can designers apply and develop them. She gave the designer the means and the inspiration. There was no aspect of the work which she did not seek to improve – working tools, materials, methods. As far back as 1850, in her first publication, she produced a little pattern which embodies the whole state of tatting in that year, largely achieved by herself. This little motif, a bunch of grapes providing ornament for a man's waistcoat, and also for 'a mourning collar', had almost everything. It had indeed so much that constant reference has had to be made to it throughout this history, forerunner as it is of so many features. Incidentally it is the first recorded piece of free-style tatting, and looks entirely modern.

All but one of Riego's books has been studied for this history, and one is tempted to describe each in detail, but this would lead down too many by-paths away from the main theme. But each new feature as it occurred has been noted, with its date where possible, so that the first allusions to new construction, the introduction of crochet, gold thread, etc. are on record. The history of design, therefore, after 1850 no longer depends only on the study of existing museum pieces but on actual patterns, some of which have been worked for the illustrations in this book. Several of her methods are now obsolete, but they are all described, however briefly. Some, one is inclined to think, are worth revival.

That Riego was satisfied with her efforts is apparent in a statement published in 1866, in which she remarks: 'The favour with which Tatting in its modern form has been received, has induced me to make still further additions to the Art, and I am pleased to find that instead of its being considered a trifling and rather useless amusement, it has now become a standard branch of needlework.'

Not everyone, however, became a convert. The art of crochet had been fairly recently introduced, the invention of an Englishwoman, and on account of its comparative simplicity and speed was becoming a formidable rival, as it still is. Riego herself, and her successors, wrote many books on crochet, and therefore must have diverted some potential workers. The fact that crochet had captured the public interest was apparent to George Eliot, who was familiar with it and also tatting. In *Scenes from Clerical Life*, published in 1858, she wrote a sarcastic diatribe on 'a taste for fancy work', 'that delightful and feminine occupation', which she suggests, guarantees domestic comfort, to be sought for in a prospective bride.

'What a resource it is under fatigue and irritation to have your drawing-room well supplied with small mats, which would always be ready if you ever wanted to set anything on them. What styptic for a bleeding heart can equal copious squares of crochet, which are useful for slipping down the moment you touch them? How our fathers managed without crochet is the wonder: but I believe some poor and feeble substitute existed in their time under the name of tatting.'

A suitor of earlier days had to be satisfied if his bride-to-be could only produce a piece of tatting, on which domestic bliss rested more precariously. One hopes that this author's large public were not unduly influenced by this point of view. In those days there was little else in the way of creative work permitted to women of leisure: the fact that their energy was misdirected was scarcely their fault.

After Riego, books by English writers followed in the next decade. Mrs. Beeton, who was proficient in so many household arts besides cookery, which made her world famous, laid down the original plans for *Beeton's Book of Needlework*, which, it is stated in the preface, 'other hands have brought to a conclusion'. The first edition appeared in 1870, with over eighty pages on tatting, well illustrated with engravings.

Mrs. Beeton does not rank as one of the star pioneers, but she shows a great variety of designs and arrangements, offering many suggestions for making pieces of practical use. She was familiar with Riego's books, which she mentions, and elaborates many of her terms and methods.

Dictionary of Needlework, by S. F. A. Caulfeild and B. C. Saward, undated, but probably published a little later, contains a most comprehensive section on tatting, with as complete a survey of the craft as has been published before or since. Some of Mrs. Beeton's patterns are reproduced, and doubtless other current and earlier works have contributed. In the co-editors' opinion the word Tatting is derived from *Tattie*, the name for Indian door-mats 'of stout matting, kept wet'. There are, however, other opinions concerning the derivation of the word, which would seem to be more plausible.

A knowledge of tatting was, in fact, growing and developing in England, but how much was actually practised at this period we do not know. A temporary decline certainly followed, in spite of the high standard of the publications which were then available – standards which fell considerably in the later interpretations of the craft. No doubt simplification became necessary to encourage new workers, but much was lost during the process, in both design and technique.

If in England tatting was going into a decline towards the end of the century, this was not the case in France, from whence arose its second great exponent, a woman equally skilled in many branches of needlework and lace.

Mlle Thérèse de Dillmont

A native of Alsace, Thérèse de Dillmont had established an 'embroidery work-room' at Dornach, and in 1884 founded a publishing house in connection with it. Two years later there appeared the first edition of her famous *Ouvrages des Dames*, in French, German, Italian and English (in which language it is known as *Encyclopaedia of Needlework*).

The book includes a chapter on tatting, which she considers to be intermediate between crochet and *macramé*. She describes it as 'somewhat resembling crochet in construction', and suggests that it should be classed as 'braid work' rather than lace. Many of her early examples are edgings and insertions which themselves have the function of braids, used to trim or to join pieces of fabric. She offers a number of tatting designs, several including crochet which is itself a feature of the completed piece, rather than an accessory heading, as used by Riego.

She builds upon Riego's well-laid foundations, elaborating on the structures already known. She uses two shuttles as a matter of course, frequently with threads of several colours. The half-ring is one of her outstanding features. Here we see the name Josephine for the first time, applied to rings of single stitches (called Josephine Picots), possibly originated by her in honour of Napoleon's Empress. Many ways are suggested for using the work, which under her hands shows its great potentialities.

Dillmont did not live to know that her book was selected as one of the forty French publications 'reputed to be most useful in women's education' at the Chicago Exhibition of 1893, for she died in 1890. Nevertheless her work and name live on, for the large number of subsequent editions all bear her name, as they do to this day.

If her book had the following it deserved, tatting must again have reached one of its peaks. It cannot, however, have been taken very seriously in England, for by the turn of the century and after, the coarse, crude examples which came to be produced showed a sad relapse from the fine early Victorian pieces. Some workers persisted in the more delicate designs, and to them we owe the very continuance of the craft in this country; but the majority of the surviving productions were monotonous and uninspired, clumsy in execution, and hardly deserving of the title of lace.

Again the craft was rescued from its depression, and again by no less than Royalty.

H.M. the Queen of Roumania

Queen Marie of Roumania was an accomplished and creative artist in the work. She and her friend Lady Hoare combined in producing a book *The Art of Tatting*, published in 1910, usually known as Lady Hoare's Book. It is not a pattern book, but consists mainly of illustrations of their original work. The introduction, which is written by the Queen, contains the following passage:

'The solitary woman, who has time for reading and thinking – and there are many – may find pleasure in imitating some of our inventions and in adding some inventions of her own.' She continues: 'Tatting has the charm of lacemaking and weaving combined. It is the same shuttle as in the weaving loom, only the loom is our fingers and the shuttle obeys our thoughts and the invention of the moment. The joy when a new stitch is found is very great.'

Her Majesty's contribution to the craft, and her unique application of the many pieces she made, is a milestone in tatting evolution. Some of her pieces are described later in the text.

Lady Hoare

'In all the notices on Tatting that I can find there seems to be no idea that anything but circles, ovals, or adaptations of circles, can be made. But with two shuttles and an inventive brain, there is no end to the designs that may be invented', observed Lady Hoare, whose own inventive ability and shuttles were put to such advantage that a constant stream of new ideas and work flowed from both one and the other. Of the shuttles she had complete mastery: she used them as an artist uses a crayon, to depict the shape that she intended. Under her hands the ring and chain took on new attitudes: working on the old basic shapes she moved them into new relationships.

Her book gives several pages of what she calls 'simple insertions and patterns' and it is in these collections of 'scraps', which serve as an artist's preliminary sketches, that her ideas take shape and form. It is probable, too, that tatting owes much of its present style to these scraps, as she shows many rudimentary forms of motifs now well established. To us, they look a little untidy: loosely defined and lacking in precision. But it is the ideas behind them that count, the fact that they are breaking away from the universally used medallion, effected by a more intelligent use of the chain: it was given a chance, as it were, almost for the first time in its history to do something more than connect one motif to another, for which it was originally designed. Had the book been less expensive, and accompanied by actual working directions, there is no doubt that it would have been eagerly secured by more workers of the time who would have been fired by her imagination and vision. As it is, it is a connoisseur's book, for the experienced worker.

In the meantime, the work in France must have been going steadily forward, for a small volume, *La Frivolité*, was published in 1924 at a price within reach of all. One of de Dillmont's pupils, Mlle Alice Morawska, an Austrian, produced a selection of advanced designs based on the work of her late teacher. The author, like all the other writers, refers to the eighteenth century, when *Frivolité* 'was in great vogue', and describes how, after a period of neglect, it was again in favour. This revival, she said, was justified by virtue of the simplicity and creative character of the work. 'Our models, of extreme fineness, are composed of rings and chains of different sizes, well proportioned and harmoniously disposed.' As indeed they were. Her medallions, called 'Rosaces', and recommended to be employed as 'incrustations' are masterpieces of ingenuity, precision and elaboration. This was the best book France had yet produced: to the tatting designer and worker it still is, owing its original inspiration as it does to the famous French pioneer.

From this brief account of the four torch-bearers of tatting, we see the revival, or perhaps establishment (but not the origin) of the craft in England, France, Germany, and possibly Italy. It does not, however, account for the fact that tatting is, or has been, in so very many countries of the world. Therefore the existence of other equally gifted workers, interested in tatting development, cannot be precluded. If they did exist, they may have evolved their own methods spontaneously, or they may have been in touch with the countries afore-mentioned, for tatting travels not unlike a plant, whose seeds have many methods of migration. And travel it did, through visiting missionaries to the East, who taught it in convent schools, and early settlers who developed it in the U.S.A. and Australia.

Once established, it took root, and like all plants transplanted, it has taken on a slightly different look from its parent in the foreign soil. This is because the taste, heritage of skill and requirements differ with race and geographical position, although in a few more years this statement will barely apply! Many of the countries into which it was absorbed and developed gave it an individual name.

Some of its titles

The English word 'Tatting' is said to be derived from the Icelandic *Taeta* – which indicates little pieces of wool combings. It also means to tease, knot, or pick up. Tatting is built up of little pieces which in earlier practice were sewn together to make one piece of fabric. The expression 'rags and tatters' denoted in medieval times a beggar's dress, hanging in rags and little pieces. A tatterdemalion was a man so attired. The word tatting was presumably applied to the work to denote its (apparent) fragility and composition: in fact, its lace-like quality.

Some other languages also name it for its appearance, the old Italian *Occhi* for example, meaning 'little eye' which the classic rings resemble. The ring is such a basic shape that it could be considered symbolic of very many forms of nature, according to the direction of the imagination of the observer. One of the Finnish words – there are two – is *Karriko*, which also means 'reef of rocks'. A large part of Finland consists of rock-studded lake, the rocks just appearing at intervals as a reef. A row of rings somewhat resembles a reef – possibly the word for this familiar object was transferred to the work. The other Finnish word, and in more common use, is *Sukkulapitsi*: sukkula meaning 'shuttle', and pitsi denoting 'lace'. Pitsi is transferred into the Estonian language (which country received a Finnish migration) in *Sustikpitsikudumine*.

Words denoting the shape of the shuttle, rather than the work itself, frequently occur, the usual example given being the German *Schiffchenarbeit* meaning 'work of the little boat', which the shuttle somewhat resembles. Many of the words are native to the language, and give their own intended meaning: but many others are simply definitions, not descriptions, meaning 'work of the shuttle', or sometimes 'lace-work'. Some are borrowed words from other languages, which presumably came into the country with the craft already established. The one word which is purely abstract is the French word *Frivolité*, although it is claimed that it also describes the character of the work. Be that as it may, accurate tatting is a serious business, and requires more patience than that usually associated with a 'frivolous' attitude. But it is not fair to translate: the French meaning of *Frivolité* cannot be exactly duplicated in English. This title is, however, rapidly excluding all the other native words as it is now in international use. It appears in almost all the current tatting books, either as the main title or as an explanatory one; sometimes it is absorbed into the language such as the Swedish *Frivolitet*. It is perhaps a pity that such an abstract definition is superseding the national names under which the work has flourished for so long in the individual countries.

The ancestry of tatting

So far we have described the course of tatting through the last two centuries, during which time it rose to heights which have not been equalled in our own day. But before this, it naturally existed in a much more primitive form, and somewhere, further back in time, it must have crystallized from rudimentary beginnings into a distinct and recognizable craft.

The tatting 'stitch' is a misnomer. Stitches are made with needles. It is, correctly, a knot, therefore developed from the very early art of knotting, and probably through *Macramé* which is the oldest of all kinds of lace. (The word 'Maqrama' is Arabic for 'fringe'.) According to Lady Hoare, such 'lace' is found in the twisted threads and knotted fringes on the wrappings of tombs in upper Egypt. Tatting is only a particular type of knotting, made with a shuttle for convenience, and this development of the early form of *macramé* was at first simply called Knotting. It came from Italy in the sixteenth century where it had been developed into a method of making mats, as well as a specialized form of lace. Additional knots were probably used in this last production, so that while it was related to tatting, it was still not pure tatting, which only consists of the one special knot, and no other. Whether this work eventually developed into pure tatting is a matter of surmise: but knotting was its early ancestor, and if this early lace did resolve into tatting, then *macramé* is also.

The evolution of a specialized form of craft, however, is not necessarily confined to only one channel. Developments in technique can take place simultaneously, from other directions, producing the same results although by different methods. The tatting knot had a long established practical application elsewhere: for example, in the art of seamanship. Possibly the modern form of tatting did not evolve from the ateliers of lace or mat makers, but from the deck of a sailing ship. Tatting is simply a fabric produced by the exploitation of its knot: anyone who used it was in a position to recognize its potentialities.

Someone presumably did, although in what precise field we do not know. Could not some seaman have observed the decorative value of an eyelet (in British seamanship the name of a (rope) ring composed of tatting knots) and given it an ornamental application in another field? Making knots in great variety was his principal occupation. An Italian sailor might have done so (there were no doubt lace-makers in his family, since lace originated in Italy) and called his new craft after the name of the eyelet, i.e. in his language 'occhi'. An early name for a very small tatted ring is 'oeillet' – which if pronounced in the English fashion would be 'eyelet' – the seagoing word. This is pure speculation, but it is not impossible that the credit for the origin of tatting as a defined craft belongs to the Italian sailor – or at least to nautical influence. All the material he needed was a coil of rope: this already lay at his feet. He was familiar with the shuttle, in the construction of fishing nets and his hammock. The fact that the craft has dispersed so widely perhaps supports this hypothesis. It would make faster progress in the hands of sailors than with lace-makers, as conditions for movement from one country to another were ideal. Lace-makers were regional and guarded jealously the mysteries of their craft: sailors moved everywhere and could spread the discovery without damaging an established means of livelihood. If such is the case, tatting, born and brought up at sea, literally sailed round the world, finding an appreciative reception in so many hands, all of which contributed to its development and flowering into a distinctive and honourable craft.

CHAPTER II

The Evolution of Tatting Design

THE TATTING KNOT

A WORKING description of the actual making of the knot over the hand, and its formation into rings and chains is given in the practical section: this appears in almost all tatting books, but a better understanding of the knot and its construction and also its possibilities is obtained by a study of the following notes, which are intended as an introduction to the principle concerned.

Various branches of the art of knotting make use of the Tatting Knot, which derives its name from its ability to form independent worked loops or eyelets, as they were originally called, which are the units of tatting. (Now described as Rings.)

If two half-hitches are tied together on an independent thread, they form a so-called double knot, i.e. made of two separate turns. If they are formed, not as a clove hitch (which is also two half-hitches) but with one turn the mirror image of the other, the resultant knot is a Lark's Head (also called a Cow Hitch).

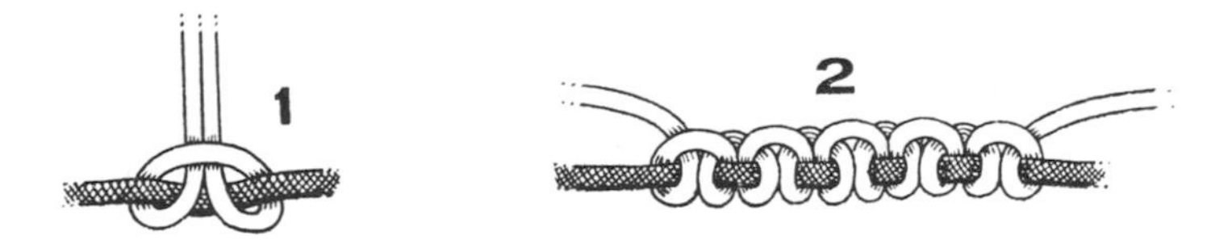

The thread upon which the knots are tied is the Running Line (in tatting often called the Foundation Thread). A running line is a thread which can be pulled from either end to shorten or lengthen it, without disturbing the knots which remain in position upon it. If a number of these knots are made upon an independent running line, the result is a tatted chain.

To form the knots on the line, use is made of the peculiar ability of the knot to transfer itself from one thread to another. The making of the knot with an endless thread (i.e. attached to a shuttle) depends on the alternation of function of the two threads. The functions are separate and distinct: the formation of the knot, and the carrying of it.

In a chain, two separate threads are used. The shuttle thread, which will be the foundation thread of the chain, temporarily gives up its use as a running line by forming the first half-hitch upon the second thread which momentarily supports it. Then by a particular 'lifting' movement the knot is turned or capsized so that it is now formed of the second thread, lying upon the shuttle thread which is now the running line again. The transition is completed. The second half-hitch is then made and transferred in the same manner, the two halves being pushed closely together to form the lark's head, or *double stitch* as it is termed in tatting.

In a ring, the principle is the same, but instead of using an independent second thread, the whole is worked by the shuttle thread of which a distant part is brought into a convenient position, so that the whole is a closed circuit. When a sufficient number of knots have been made, the running line can then be pulled tightly ('drawn up') so that the last knot will be brought round to meet the first, thus forming a closed ring.

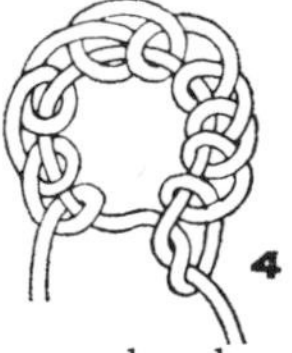

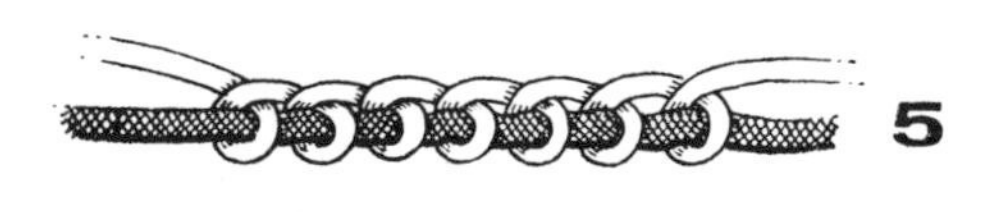

A ring can also be made of all single knots, i.e. of either one of the half-hitches. They are therefore all lying in the same direction. This is called the Josephine Ring: the example is composed of ten single knots.

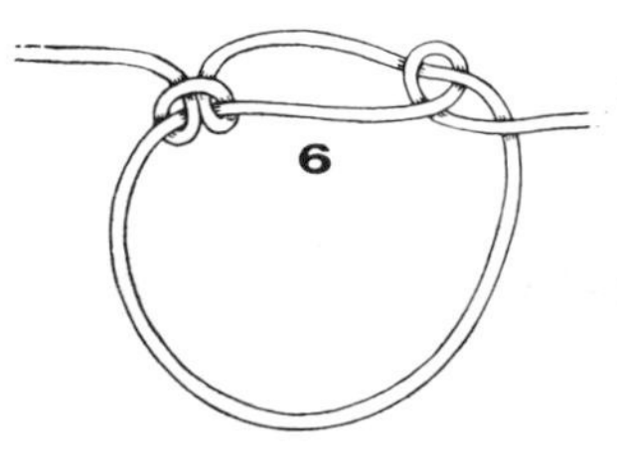

A chain can also be formed in the same manner. It is mainly theoretical and not much used.

The transference of the knot on to the running thread must be completed for every half-knot, as it is made: if one fails to be turned over, the ring cannot be drawn up, and the passage of the running thread is baulked or 'locked'. In a chain, which is not drawn into a circle, but where nevertheless the stitches are pushed up tightly together, such a lock can be made purposely to break the tension, to allow the chain to alter its direction. This is referred to as 'a locking stitch' in the text.

Figure 6 shows the beginning of a ring, with one double knot completed and the first half of another, not yet turned. When you are actually making the stitch you will not try to produce this transition stage: it is shown here simply to demonstrate what actually happens, and how the knot, before capsizing and turning, is made of the shuttle thread: it now has to be transposed so that the shuttle thread will be carrying it instead of composing it.

The picot

If one double knot is made at a slight distance from the one before it, leaving a 'space' of thread, when the knots are pushed up closely together this thread will

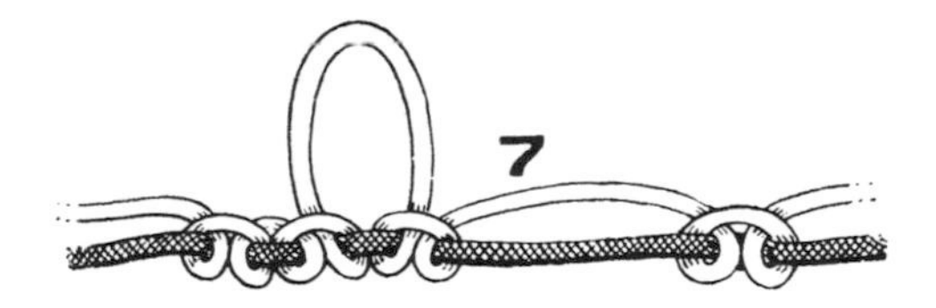

remain as a loop between the two. This is the picot. The complete double stitch is required to make it: one single stitch would slip back, and the picot would disappear. The two halves lock one another and hold together so that the loop remains.

In current English patterns, the complete knot is described as 'a double stitch'. Riego and de Dillmont contracted this to 'double', or to 'stitches', according to context. This method has been adopted in the following descriptions, as it is briefer and equally clear. The abbreviation 'DS' for double stitch, commonly used, holds good for either system of writing.

THE EVOLUTION OF TATTING CONSTRUCTION AND DESIGN

Since about the middle of the last century, tatting has consisted of its one (double) stitch, arranged either on a closed circuit – the Ring – or upon a free standing line – the Chain – which requires two threads for its construction. (Described by Lady Hoare as Single and Double tatting, since the ring requires only one shuttle for its formation.) The ring preceded the chain by several hundred years. Methods of using the ring to form simple compositions are described below.

Building rings into lines (Figs. 8–11, Plate I)

A rudimentary form of the ring is a number of stitches on a section of a running line, which is not pulled up completely, so leaving part of it unworked. This was a very early form. The original English word for it was scallop, but since this word has a much larger application it is not a suitable title. Neither is the original French word *feston* really applicable, since 'feston' is also the French word for chain. It is suggested that it be called the Half-ring. It does not at present appear in modern English patterns, but has been revived in Italy. The number of stitches composing it is optional.

The smallest number of double stitches which will satisfactorily pull into a circular ring is four, and the simplest arrangement of rings is in a straight line. These very small rings were originally known as a 'dot' or an *oeillet*.

Larger rings (in the example, twenty doubles) are pear-shaped if pulled up loosely, and become circular if they are drawn up as tightly as possible. Old names for the ring were 'loop', 'oval', 'circle', and also 'lozenge'.

The ring can be any size, but large ones do not retain their shape so well, and are difficult to pull up if the knots are very tight on the running thread.

The Josephine stitch (Figs. 12–15, Plate I)

Instead of making the ordinary pair of stitches, either the first or the second half may be used exclusively so that they 'turn' all one way. These are described as 'single' stitches and when forming a ring they bear the name 'Josephine'. Three are sometimes used to make a tiny half-ring: more stitches make a larger one. Strings of these can be used ornamentally to edge a piece of work, to give it an extra 'finish': modern Italian patterns sometimes employ it. It can also act as a rudimentary chain by connecting one group of rings to another.

Eight single stitches pulled up completely forms the Josephine Ring or Rosette, also called the Josephine Knot; but ring is a more accurate term. It was a feature of old French patterns when it was called, rather misleadingly, the Josephine Picot.

Larger Josephine rings develop a corkscrew twist – sometimes desirable though more theoretical than practical. The first half of the stitch gives the twist an anti-clockwise direction: the second half, clockwise.

Half-rings and rings, of any size, can lie on both sides of the thread by turning the work between making each ring.

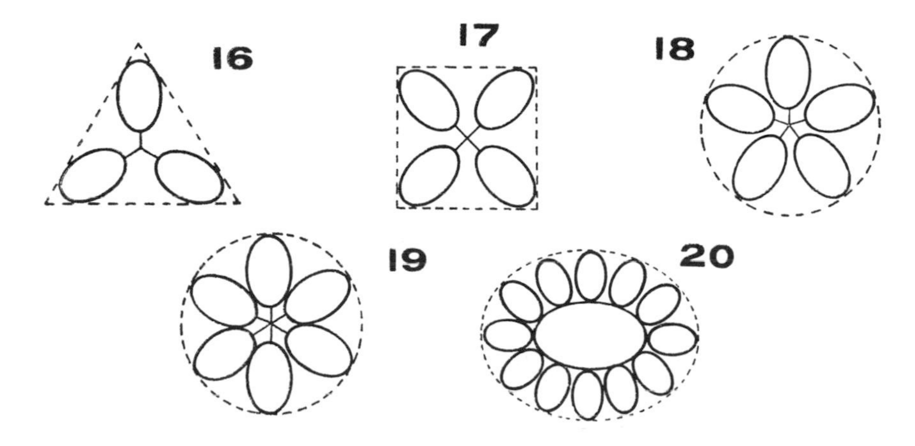

Lines into areas: basic shapes (Figs. 16–20)

The ring itself is the most primitive basic shape. It can be used in various combinations to make simple geometrical forms. A line of three or more rings can be pulled round so that the last ring meets the first, forming an enclosed space between them. The piece can be any shape, according to the number of rings used and the intention of the designer. Three rings suggest a triangle with equal sides.

Four rings suggest a square.

Five rings suggest a circle, or a pentagon, according to the final treatment of the outline.

Six rings also make a circle, or a hexagon.

A larger number can be drawn into an oval.

To produce a piece of tatted fabric, any of the above motifs may be repeated and laid in rows, each joined to the next.

Development of the basic shapes (Figs. 21–26)

Any of the basic shapes can contain additional rings to accentuate their form. For example, the triangle can consist of six rings, in two sizes. Triangles can be laid together in a number of ways. Two make a diamond shape.

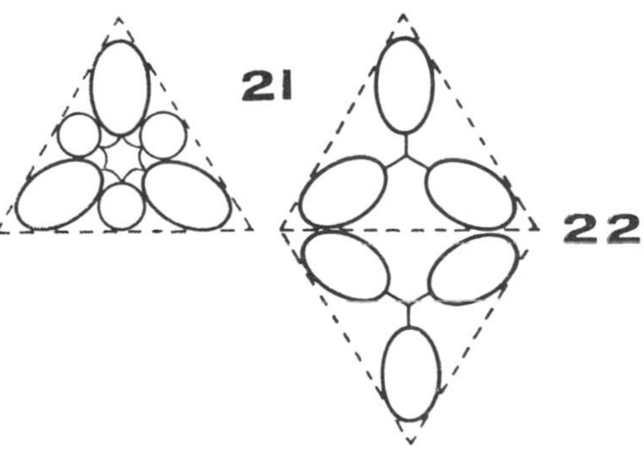

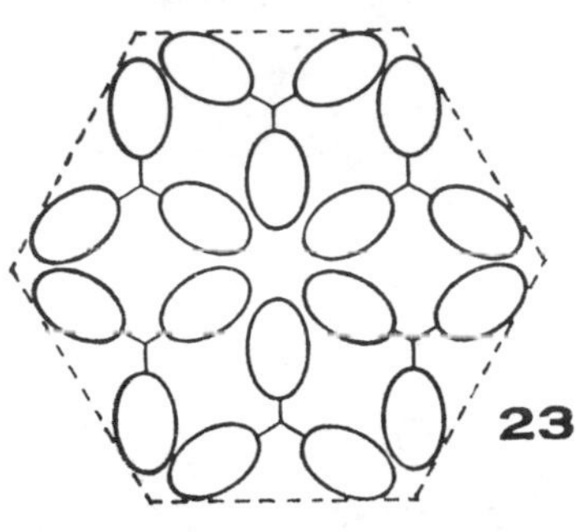

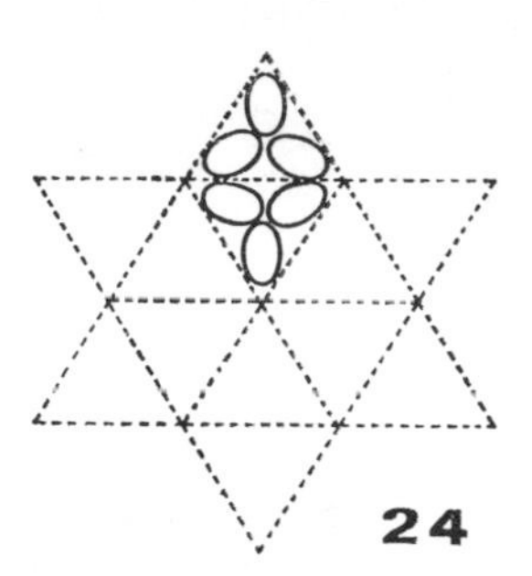

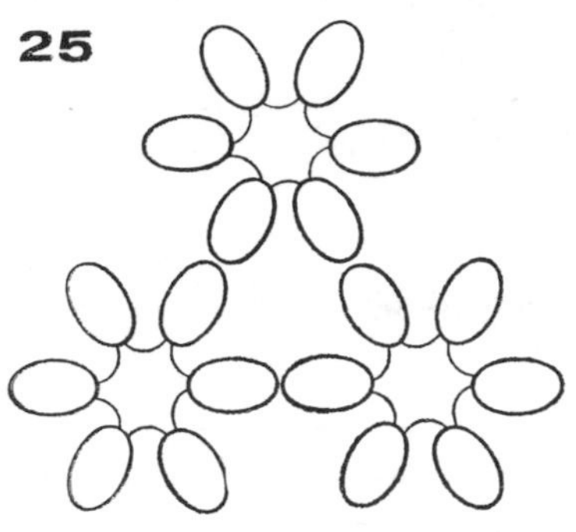

Six make a hexagon.

If another triangle is added to each of the six sides, the result is a six-point star. (The drawing is reduced in scale.)

Three six-ring circles can be combined to produce a triangular form. (One more, appropriately placed, would make a diamond. Three more, added to the diamond, would make a large circle with one in the centre.)

Such a six-ring circle, which is in effect a hexagon with six arms, can be produced in all directions, every arm linking to another to make a piece of fabric, rectangular or circular (see Plate X). A hexagon with straight sides is shown in the following figure, where circles are indicated within a large rectangular shape.

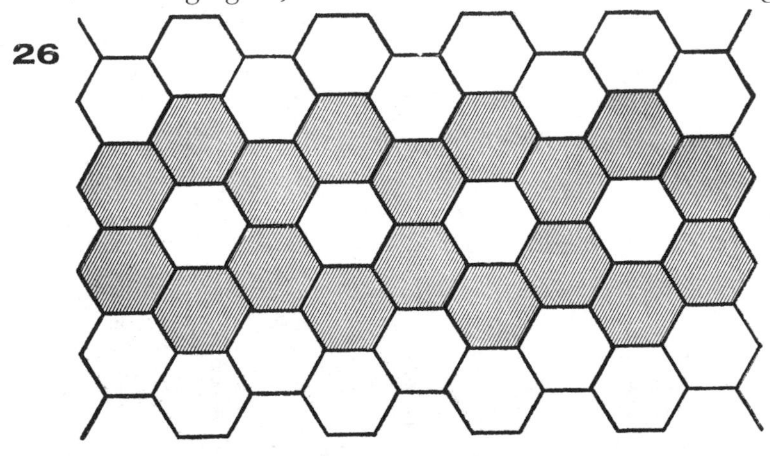

The early pieces of tatting were built up in this manner, working each motif independently. Any of the basic shapes can be added to by working other motifs around them, retaining or altering their original shape as needed.

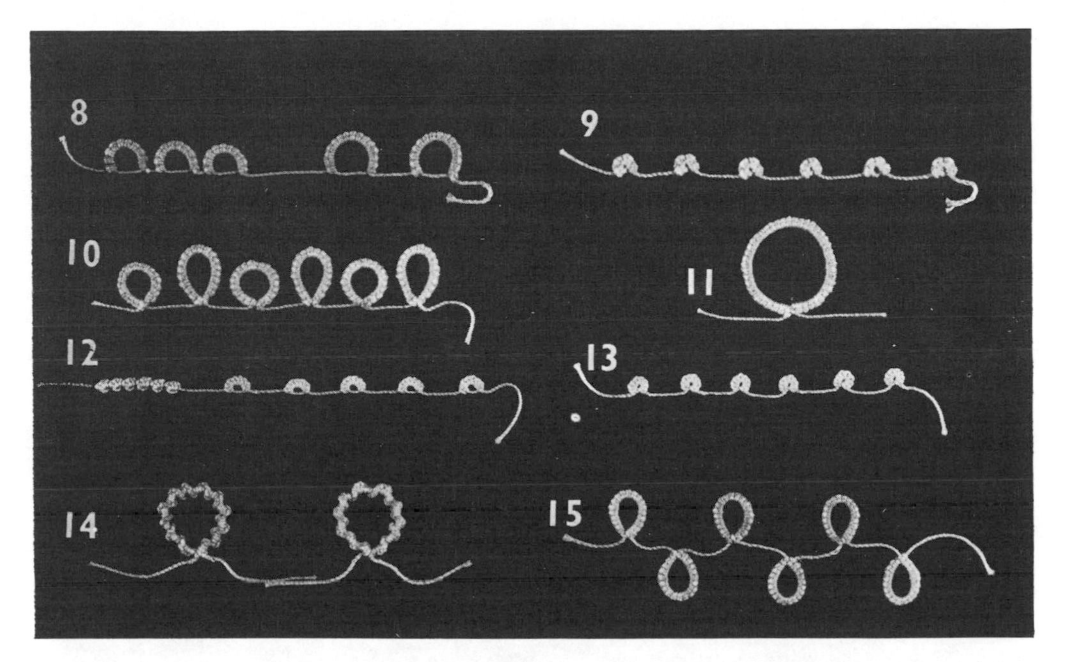

BUILDING RINGS INTO LINES · FIGURES 8–11 (*page* 22)
THE JOSEPHINE STITCH · FIGURES 12–15 (*page* 22)

THE PICOT AS ORNAMENT · FIGURES 27–32 (*page* 25)

PLATE I

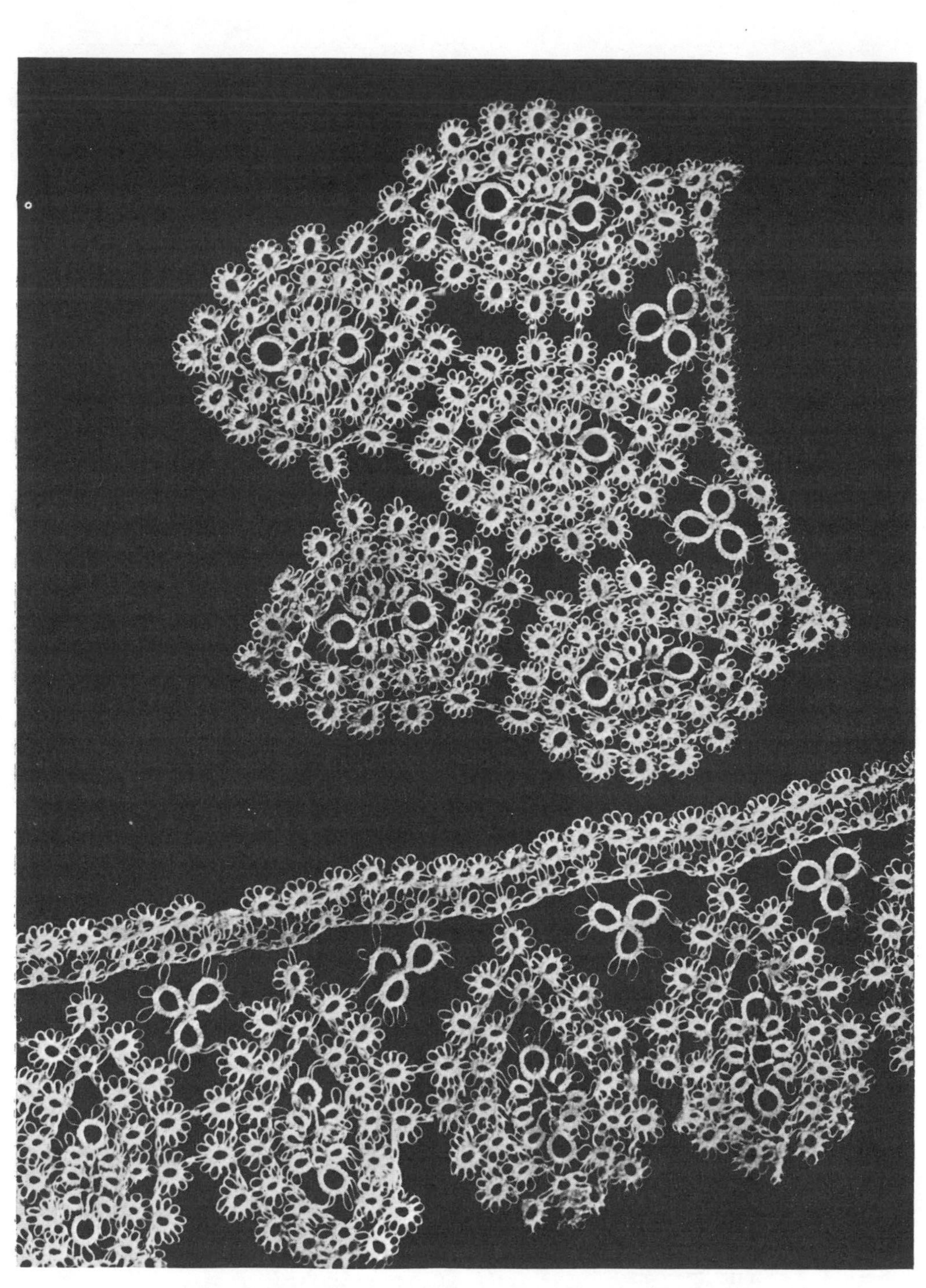

PLATE II TRIMMING ON A VICTORIAN APRON (*pages* 32, 33, 34)

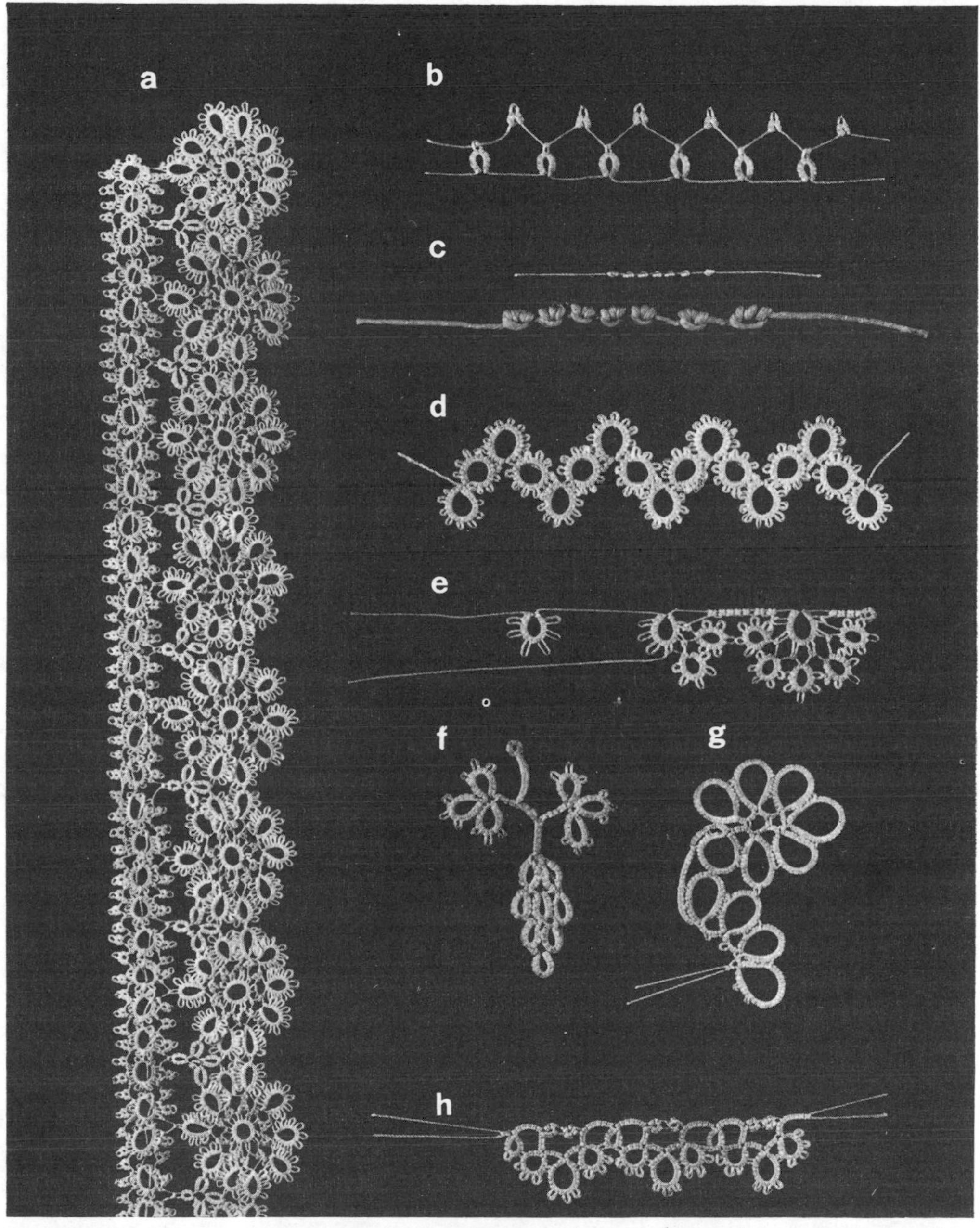

PLATE III METHODS NOW OBSOLETE (*page* 28)

a Collar, oriel pattern, worked with needles (*page* 29) · **b** The use of the needle for static joins (*page* 28) · **c** A string of 'knotting' (*page* 37) · **d** Vandyke edging: 'passing the thread behind' (*page* 37) · **e** Rings round a 'centre' (*page* 29), also shows a nearly continuous thread and a false chain (*page* 38) · **f** The bunch of grapes, perfect continuous thread but false chain (*page* 39) · **g** Mandarin sleeve trimming, false chain (*page* 39) · **h** Narrow edging, true chain, modern method, two shuttles (*page* 41)

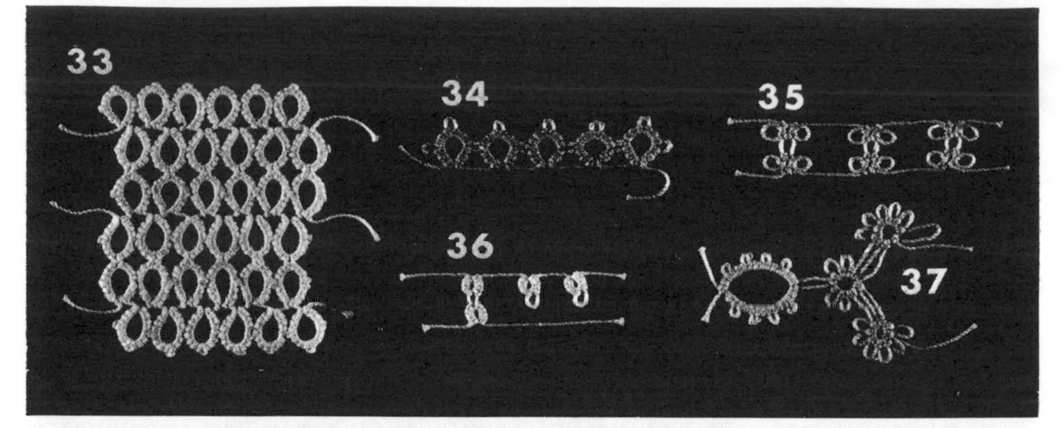

THE PICOT AS A JOINING AGENT · FIGURES 33–37 (*page* 31)

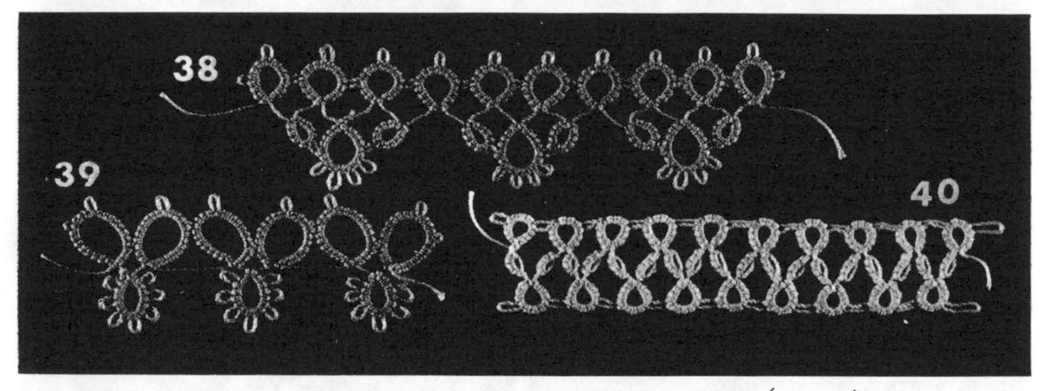

EDGINGS FROM RINGS ALONE · FIGURES 38–40 (*page* 32)

THE CLOVER, DAISY, AND THE WHEEL (classic formations) · FIGURES 41–44 (*page* 32)

PLATE IV

CHAPTER III

The Picot

THE picot forms so much a part of tatting that it must be described at this early stage. Rather curiously, its use as ornament preceded that of function, i.e. a means of joining, by several hundred years. Present-day picots are made as described in Figure 7. Riego's first picots were made between the first and second halves of the same stitch, instead of between two double stitches, but the effect is very much the same.

THE PICOT AS ORNAMENT (Figs. 27–32, Plate I)

The picot gives a lighter, lace-like quality to the rings and was used in great profusion in Victorian work. A ring carrying many picots was sometimes known as a 'rosette'. As a rule the picot is comparatively short, but it can be made any length. At the moment they appear to be becoming longer. Picots used to be measured over a 'tatting or purling pin': these pins were available in various numbered sizes. An old name for the picot was a 'purl', 'pearl' or 'pearl loop', and an 'extra pearl' was one of double the normal length. If picots are reasonably short, and of the same size, practice enables them to be formed by eye: but if a series of graduated lengths is needed, or a large number of long ones, it will be necessary to measure them on a gauge. Very long ones (up to $1\frac{1}{2}$ inches in length when drawn up) are used in flower patterns.

The picot can be made between every double stitch, or less frequently, according to the effect required. At its simplest, it is shown between every (double) stitch on the smallest ring.

On a larger ring, between every double, it gives the impression of a little frill.

Between every two doubles the individual picots are more distinct.

With a larger number of stitches between (in the example, five doubles) the effect is balanced and restrained.

Since length is a matter of degree, there can be no precise division between what is normal and what is not. Where, however, they are obviously quite long, for a specific purpose, they can be described as 'a long picot': its actual measured length depends on the designer and worker.

The long picot

A ring of nine doubles, carrying eight measured picots of equal size.

Here is a modern piece, a ring bearing decorative picots equally spaced and graduated in length, like a Baroque sunburst.

Joining one ring to another: some early methods

Lines and circles of rings cannot go on indefinitely without some method of holding them together. A line of rings needs to be attached to the one above or below it: an outer circle must be joined to an inner one to form a medallion. Several methods were used before the one now in common practice, i.e. integrating the join into the work as it proceeds.

1. Probably the first method was needle and thread. Round or square medallions were sewn together forming rows, to make up a fabric. The needle might pass either through a picot or round the thread on which the rings were carried.

2. Later, two picots, each on a separate ring, were tied together with an additional thread and the ends cut off. This must have been tedious in the extreme. Both these methods, however, had the advantage of being able to work each piece independently, therefore keeping them cleaner and fresher, laying them aside on completion until all were finished and ready to assemble.

The trimming on a Victorian apron, shown in Plate II, illustrates both. The illustration shows a pocket and part of the trimming up the side: the foundation is black silk. The principal motif of the design is an oval medallion, which was composed of three separate rows of rings. The first and inner row consists of two large circular rings, separated by three smaller ones. This line of rings is drawn into an oval, as in the manner described in Figure 20. The enclosed space so produced was later filled in with needlework. The second row of rings, which are of identical size, is worked independently and then attached to picots on the first row by a needle and thread (of the same material). The needle is passed through a picot on the row beneath it, and then through two other picots, left and right (one each from two adjoining rings) knotting all three picots together. The thread is then carried to the next picot on the row beneath, thus working round until the second row of rings is securely in position. The third and outer row, consisting of slightly larger rings, and naturally more of them, is applied in the same manner.

The second method, tying the picots together, was used to unite the ovals, each oval now being a complete unit. In the photograph it can be seen where some of the knots have broken away. The ovals were also tied to little picot-bearing triangular motifs, which filled up spaces between them. A double row of rings was then sewn (by method 1) on to the ovals and triangles. (It is assumed that this apron was made about 1840.)

Tying picot to picot was the standard method used in France, where patience was apparently unlimited. The pieces were laid face down on shaped paper and sewn into position, before tying. Such a system did not satisfy Riego, who, on introducing the work to her English public remarks: 'In this state it has recently been revived in France, under the title of *Frivolité*.' (One wonders what the French called it originally.) With a complete disregard for any previous English writers, she continues:

'I have been much solicited for some time past to introduce the work in England, and have delayed doing so until I could simplify the mode of working and endeavour to render it suitable to the taste of the English lady.' Some method must be found which would eliminate the time-consuming tying of knots. The problem was to pass the shuttle thread through the picot: the shuttle itself obviously could not. Riego responded to the challenge by simply discarding the shuttle.

Her own words, in the preface to her first publication, *The Tatting Book* (1850), describe her method: 'To obviate the difficulties above mentioned I have substituted a netting needle for the shuttle which has enabled me to attach and shape the pattern while working: and where the loops are too small to admit of the netting needle passing through, I have given directions for using a sewing needle instead.'

The netting needle was 6–7 inches in length and must have been of extreme fineness to pass, when loaded, through a picot; but pass it did; and judging by the fineness of the thread she used, a very small picot at that.

She gives two methods of joining, the first to be used while working, joining a ring under construction to a picot on a ring already made (the modern principle but a more primitive method). The running thread (she calls it the foundation thread) is passed through the picot via the needle, and as she says, 'care must be taken that the joining does not prevent the foundation thread from drawing'. After carrying the thread through the picot, the ring can be resumed in the normal manner.

It was not, however, always necessary or desirable to join ring to ring. The needle might be employed in making a second row (on an edging) or a 'round', when drawing up was not required. In fact what was needed was just the opposite, a firm anchorage for the centre of a 'space' of thread at a picot where it was to be held permanently. Here she uses her second method, employing a fine sewing needle. She makes what she calls 'an overcast stitch', passing the needle twice through the picot and knotting firmly into it. The needle of course has to be on an uncomfortably long stretch of thread (at least 1½ yards) if joins are to be avoided in any but a small piece of work. An example of this practice is shown in Plate IIIb.

Note on Plate III a to k

The examples shown in Plate III are all early patterns, worked by methods which are now obsolete. They are therefore not included amongst the numbered figures of the text. Reference will be made to them as and when they show the particular feature under discussion. The original illustrations for these patterns are engravings from imaginary drawings, in other words they represent theoretical perfection. This presents some difficulty in working a reproduction, for such a drawing is not proof that the piece has actually been worked, or is even workable, whereas a photograph is. Neither does it instruct, i.e. show beginnings and endings, or, more important, sequence of joining, which a correctly drawn working diagram does. Both are needed to give a complete picture of an elaborate piece, if it is to be copied. The imaginary drawing fails on both counts: it often contains fewer or more stitches than the pattern describes, and is out of proportion. The utmost care therefore has been taken by more than one experienced worker in the study of these patterns, which employ terms no longer used, and whose engravings are sometimes so small as to render some essential details invisible.

To illustrate the use of the needle, as described above, a straight strip of work is shown: the lower row consists of a line of rings bearing picots: the thread of the upper row anchors into a picot on the row beneath, and after leaving a short space of thread, makes another small picot-bearing ring: another short space, then joins into the next picot on the lower round. (The fact that the picot shows, indicates the order in which the rounds were made: compare this with Figure 92 to which it has a superficial resemblance.)

A discovery is worth double when its application can be extended to further developments. With her needles, Riego was able to make advanced shapes ahead of her time, even if 'improperly' constructed. She immediately applied the discovery to the making of medallions, and although we have not yet arrived at their description (made with picots joined in the modern manner) one of her examples is given here since it shows so clearly its development from the new method. She realized that in the above example was the nucleus of a new formation, i.e. a central ring to which other rounds could be attached. The line of rings, as worked, could be brought round to form a circle – but better still one ring bearing picots could replace it.

An edging, shown in Plate IIIe, gives a transition stage, where a row of rings is worked partly round and joined to a ring in the 'centre'. The last step was to surround the centre completely. This she did in her design for 'a collar, oriel pattern', which is a particularly graceful illustration of the principle, shown in Plate IIIa.

It is composed of a row of thirteen such medallions (called 'stars'): the central ring of a star is followed by two rounds, the single thread unbroken throughout. The first round is as the second row of rings in Plate IIIb: the second and final round carries fairly large rings with picots between every two doubles. The stars are connected by small 'diamonds' at the neck edge. The neck band (a row of rings head to tail) is bordered by tiny rings carried on the thread, which anchors on the lower side into appropriate picots of the stars and diamonds. In the absence of a netting needle it was made entirely with an ordinary darning needle. Here then is a medallion in advance of those produced hitherto: the many spaces of thread in the interior and neck-band give it a feeling of lightness and delicacy, without additional needlework. In other patterns made in the same manner the 'spaces' are often more dominant than the rings, which are made the minimum size. It was the era of 'spaces', which lasted until the solid chain replaced them.

This pattern, together with some half-dozen others, all composed with needles, appears in her first book: by using the needle instead of the shuttle the stitch became one of those used in Point Lace. With this additional description tatting was now glorified, yet simplified, and in Riego's view, more suited to the English public.

In the meantime, other workers had been pursuing the same problem, the problem might one say of passing the camel through the needle's eye. There were other equally industrious workers in the field. In the following year, 1851, a modest writer, who describes herself simply as 'a Lady', provided the solution in a little booklet, *Tatting made Easy, and how to join with the shuttle explained and exemplified.* And therein she describes, very simply, the modern method: 'Lay the loop under the pearl to which it is to be joined.' The loop is then pulled through, and the shuttle passed through the loop. 'Then complete the second half of the stitch.' This she calls 'The Joining Stitch'. Her picots are made as we make them today – between pairs of double stitches. She makes no personal claim to the discovery: she just describes it.

The Lady's method was the better one, but she had not Riego's vision. Not only did Riego see the possibilities of the joined picot (both methods, running and static), she immediately developed them. The Lady offers not much more than her book title states; her few patterns consist of four edgings (all half-rings of different sizes) and what she calls 'Couvrettes' – rectangular pieces of tatting composed either of edging worked upon edging, or of the simplest medallions, of rings enclosing a space. They do little more than demonstrate the normal joining of the picot to the working thread. The keynote of the whole book is simplicity: it is a masterpiece of concise writing. In teaching the stitch (not attempted by Riego) she uses three illustrations of the knot only: no shuttle, no hands. Working directions, which become longer in every modern publication, are brevity itself, yet presumably sufficient.

We do not know if Riego and 'a Lady' became aware of one another's work. A second edition of Riego's book appears in 1852, but there is no mention of it then. She may of course have arrived at the discovery independently, at a later date. But it was not until 1861, nine years later, when she published her second book, *Tatting: Edgings and Insertions*, that she describes it. In her preface she says: 'This fashionable Art has been little used for the purpose to which it is now applied, as by the previous method, it wanted firmness and strength, but by a careful study of the work, and a new method of joining this difficulty is obviated, and these patterns will be found as durable and wash as well as those in crochet or knitting.'

She then describes the modern method in simple and precise terms. She is now forming the picot as the Lady formed it, between pairs of double stitches, instead of splitting a double stitch. She has also invented a metal ring, to be worn on the left thumb, to which is attached the purling pin, which was also used to pry the loop through the picot. She has reverted to the shuttle: there is no further mention of needles, in this book or in any subsequent one.

Quite probably her system of needles did not last very long. It could never be entirely satisfactory anyway. Admittedly, it was not necessary to carry about a crochet hook, as it is today, but it must have been slow work drawing the netting needle through a picot, and making the actual stitch with any kind of needle (especially on a very long thread) can never be as quick as with a shuttle. The 'Needle Period' can really only be considered as transitional, and its real value lay in showing the way to new designs, which could be carried out when the needle became obsolete. Once the new method was made known it must have become universal quite quickly. Other countries where tatting was practised which did not have access to Riego's book, probably by-passed the needle stage altogether, and indeed have worked out the modern method on their own. Joining by picot was the current problem of the age, and must have been every worker's concern at that time.

THE PICOT AS JOINING AGENT (Figs. 33–37, Plate IV)

The picot used in joining may be any size. Its length will determine the final distance between the two pieces. If very small it will not show, and the two rings will appear simply to meet at that point. This little picot is much used in flower-work, and patterns using it describe it as the 'link' picot. Here, where rings stand on both sides of the thread (as in Fig. 15) three such rows of rings have been joined invisibly to one another, and each ring to its neighbour, left and right.

Picots of average size

If large enough to show (the usual size) they appear between the two rings, an additional decoration. Figure 30, with its spaced picots, develops into Figure 34.

If two rows of Figure 27 (the smallest ring, bearing three picots) are worked independently, and placed head to head, and the centre picot of the first row is engaged by the ring in the second row (during working) the result is rather unusual.

Josephine rosettes can carry picots if one of the stitches lies the opposite way, to lock it in place.

Picots of greater length than normal

Sometimes the design calls for a longer picot. It may need to be longer to join another motif that is just out of reach, or conversely it may be required to push another farther away, to prevent overcrowding and overlapping of rings. Both are shown here in the same illustration. A large ring, bearing eight small picots and one extra long one, is connected by it to an independent row of rings which lies beneath it. Each of the small rings in the row below is pushed slightly apart from its neighbour, and at the same time joined to it, by an extra-long picot. One is visible on the ring at the right. Arrangements of the picot are almost inexhaustible: some of the newer ways of using it are described later in the text.

CHAPTER IV

The Ring

UNTIL about the middle of the last century, all tatting designs were composed of rings alone. Extraordinary ingenuity was displayed in their arrangement, the only means of variation being their size, relative position, and the number and size of the picots they carried. To allow progression from one point to another, all compositions include 'spaces' of unworked thread, of varying lengths, i.e. of the thread on which the rings stand. The simplest groupings are of course, edgings: these can consist of one 'round' only, or several, thus producing deep bands of trimming. More complicated edgings are described later; for present purposes three are shown here, each consisting of one round only (Figs. 38–40, Plate IV). All are developed from Figure 15 where the rings stand on both sides of the thread.

This well-known design is quick and easy to make: the arrangement of the rings is such that the effect is as if it were composed of two rounds.

This is a modern Italian pattern, good in fine thread.

Old French. This is really an insertion – both edges the same. It illustrates what only one size of ring, and one half-ring can do in a single round, without ornament.

Many other edgings can of course be produced from rings alone: any number of rounds can be worked. The Victorian apron shows an edging, consisting of a single row (and also one of a double row) of identical rings, each bearing many rather long picots.

SOME CLASSIC FORMATIONS (Figs. 41–44, Plate IV)

The clover. There are a number of formations of rings which are so well known, and occur so often, that they have been given a name. One of these is the 'Clover', a group-

linked together, as shown in Figure 41.
name and treated as a unit: it is one of
ne principal motif in a pattern, or it can
motifs, at the same time filling in an
apron the triangular motif illustrates
: clover, since the rings are all the same

a description of edgings leads naturally
two figures, the Daisy and the Wheel,
so both classical formations.
a circle is made from a line of rings,
ner in which the early medallions were
, not standing alone, but attached to a
ne centre. It carries the required number
will surround it (generally eight). The
ontrol the size of the central ring.
s is worked straight on to it. The thread
knotted into it as closely as possible and
ad is then drawn through the next picot,
. The rings are joined to one another by
ra picot for ornament, or for attachment
round is worked it would have to be
s the final stitch of the daisy brings the
it off. As it stands, it is recognized as the
oup of medallions where the central ring
, three out of the eight rings have been

ot counting the central ring as a round),
classic wheel. Here the central ring is
e cut off on completion. It often carries
tion of Figure 15 (rings on both sides of
ects with the picots on the central ring:
ner, according to the design. These inner
in the opposite direction, on the other
may be large or small, may or may not be

connected to one another; but whatever their shape and size, this round still represents its prototype (Fig. 15). An inner ring is made first: a space of thread is left before the outer ring is worked: an equal space of thread, and then the second inner ring is made, thus proceeding right round in a zig-zag fashion, to produce the complete wheel. The illustration shows a central ring of twelve picots: the spaces of thread in this design are rather short. The round attached to it is worked to just over half-way. This 'half-wheel', exactly as worked, is often used as a border, giving the effect of scallops.

We have seen the application of the longer picot in Figure 37 where a row of picot-bearing rings are joined together, giving a comfortable space between them. Such a row is often added to the wheel. In the following example, the central ring is exactly the same as in the wheel shown above, but the inner rings are very small and are not joined to one another. The spaces of thread between them and the outer rings are much longer, and the outer rings are small: they are like Figure 27, but beginning and ending with two doubles instead of one, to give slightly more body. They are not joined to one another. The row added is only partially worked, to show the construction more clearly (see also Fig. 37). The thread connecting the rings is knotted into the centre picot of the outer rings of the wheel. The long picot is visible on the last ring made, and also on the first, as since the row is to be a circle, it will be required by the last ring which will connect with it.

This additional round can also be worked independently, and sewn on with needle and thread after completion (in the manner of the Victorian ovals). Made in this way, the sewing thread will pass through the appropriate picot on the wheel, and although the rings in this new round (unlike the Victorian ovals) are already joined by the long picot, it is passed twice round the centre of this picot, embracing also the basic thread on which the rings stand, thus binding all the threads together at one point, rather like a little bundle of sticks. This round lies flatter if sewn on than worked on, is neater and more compact in spite of the additional sewing thread, and is generally more satisfactory, besides being easier to work.

The wheel made exactly as described does not appear in Mlle de Dillmont's book *Frivolité*. She uses Figure 15, rings on both sides of the line (see Fig. 68 described later), drawn into a circle, and a central ring, but never the two together. The wheel, however, was known by 1897, if not before. In a revised edition of the *Times Century Dictionary*, published in that year, an illustration of Figure 43 is shown.

The wheel represents an evolutionary step towards modern tatting, and is perhaps the climax of the ring formations. It could be quickly made, since the round following the central ring covered a good deal of space. It was in effect, two rounds in one, and therefore an advance on Riego's stars, in which the two rounds had to be worked separately. It lends itself to considerable variation through the size and shape of its rings, 'spaces' of thread, and picots, and now appears in many modern pattern books.

So satisfying is the ring as the sole basic motif, so lace-like and delicate can be the result, that most present-day tatting books show some patterns still made of the ring alone, which many workers prefer exclusively.

CHAPTER V

The Search for a New Form

AT sometime, perhaps in several places, workers must have felt the need for further development in tatting design. Going round in circles was all very well, but they had been doing just that for several hundred years, and it had its limitations. It is not a progressive movement: the thread ends where it begins, at the base of the ring. It is a 'tied' thread and cannot branch off independently: the ring is a closed circuit. In any piece of fabric made as described under basic shapes, there are constant beginnings and endings, with cut threads to finish off out of sight. Obviously the ring was a handicap: what was needed was a row of stitches which need not be drawn up but could remain a straight (or curved) line, able to branch off in any direction, for any length.

Several ingenious attempts were made to simulate this. The problem of joining one motif to another had originally been solved either by tying, or, more advanced, by a string of 'knotting'. In Riego's own words:

' "Knotting", which is also an ancient work, may be termed a variation of Tatting, as it is made with a shuttle, and was used to attach that work together when it was made in little pieces, but which my improvements have rendered unnecessary. Still, as it is useful in joining and as all arts formerly practiced must be interesting at the present day, I now give instructions for it.'

The 'knot' in question consisted of three turns of the thread upon a loop which was then drawn up in the manner of a half-ring. A row of these was made to measure, which could link into threads upon which rings were carried: where necessary it could carry a ring itself. Here in effect was a free line of a kind: as a rudimentary chain it served very well, for not only did it join two pieces together, it was also a means of carrying the thread to a distant point, and that was the object in view, while it had the added advantage of being decorative in itself. (A string of 'knots' is shown in Plate IIIc.) As the knots are so small, even in No. 20 thread, a similar row worked in string is also shown.

An early method of getting the thread to another part of the work, and invisibly, was to pass it behind a ring just made, letting it lie along one side of the ring so that it did not show on the upper surface, and then starting a new ring from the point reached. Rings could therefore lie in a straight band, head to tail, instead of upright. The thread of course had to be secured to (or near) the apex of the previous one, a position which was rather misleadingly called 'the centre'. Sometimes it was linked into the ring itself (as in the neck-band of the collar in Plate III). Here Riego forced the sewing needle through the worked line, or passed it through the ring, as she proceeded. When, later, she reaches the stage of passing the thread (on a shuttle) through a picot, she provides one for the purpose.

Even after the discovery of the chain, Riego still used this method, as it produced an effect which nothing else can, but the passage of the thread becomes more complicated. Sometimes, after passing through a picot, the thread is extended into space, before making a second ring which is connected during its making to a picot on the last ring made. In other words, the two rings are joined head to head. As a variation, in one of her patterns, the thread leaves from the side of a ring instead of the opposite end. With so much licence in the passage of the thread it was possible to produce quite broad bands of one round, the rings set at many angles. In these patterns the spaces of thread are rather dominant and the work would be very fragile. Eventually the chain replaced the spaces, and such contortions of the thread were no longer necessary. The last example she gave is a pattern for a vandyke edging which is a variation of 'passing the thread behind'. Here she sets the rings, rigidly, in short rows to form angles of approximately 45 degrees. Pairs of rings are made, facing away from one another (tail to tail). The thread is then passed behind the second of the pair, and through a picot, to be in position for making the next pair, for which the work is reversed. The ring at the apex of the vandyke is joined to the ring preceding it, and also to the one which follows, thus forming the angle. It is shown in Plate IIId.

The vandyke edging is capable of considerable variation and development and can make attractive pieces, both straight and circular. In one early pattern it was worked independently, drawn into a circle and then joined by strings of knotting to a previously worked centre motif, the whole to be followed by an outer round. The final result is a circular piece described as 'Round D'Oyley or Head-dress'.

Queen Marie, who evidently preferred the use of rings alone, made many pieces which appear to be made of a number of independent groups of rings, but were really composed all on one thread without a join, by manipulating the thread behind the work. Lady Hoare gives a description of her method:

'She has a small hook on a chain fastened to her dress, and she draws the thread with the hook along through the stitches behind until she reaches the desired spot: by this means she can begin her pattern again.'

'Passing the thread behind' is now obsolete, but it might well be re-introduced where the straight or angular band is required, as it is firm, neat and attractive.

The false chain

The next (and last) stage before the chain finally evolved was the production of what might be called a 'false' or 'improper' chain. It was a real chain, but the means of producing it were false, i.e. it was not tatted by the shuttle. This method is now obsolete, but what a gift it is to the free-style designer!

Riego shows a very ingenious example in her first book (1850) when she almost reached the method of the continuous thread. To make an edging, she works a number of picot-bearing rings, spacing them an inch apart. When a sufficient number have been worked for the required length of the edging, she leaves a half-inch space of thread and works a small oeillet – this is to provide a neat finish. Now she turns back: she wants to reach the last ring made, but is half an inch distant from it. She works what she calls 'an overcast stitch' on this half-inch, for about three-quarters of its length. In all the patterns in this book she is working with needles, but a shuttle would have been equally possible to form the stitches. She says: 'The overcast stitches in these directions are worked in the ordinary manner: the thread from the needle forms the stitch, and the thread of the material upon which it is worked the foundation: in the tatting it is the reverse.'

She has in fact produced a tatted chain, but since the second thread (the half-inch space) is fixed at both ends, it cannot itself form the knot; therefore she has produced a tatted chain, but not by tatting, which is the actual transference of the knot from one thread to another. To continue the edging, on arrival within a convenient distance of the last ring made on the line, she works five rings round it, passing the needle through its picots. (This figure has already been used to demonstrate a build-up round a central ring.) After joining into the last picot on the so-called 'central' ring she meets the inch space of thread, upon which she works overcast stitches as before, for about two-thirds of its length. The scallop is now repeated, round the next free-standing ring. Historically this is an important piece, as it shows not only her first attempt at a worked chain, but also a nearly 'continuous' thread, and the 'central' ring to which another round is attached. A partially worked strip of edging is shown in Plate IIIe. The piece was begun at the left, and on the return journey is of course worked from right to left.

Her next attempt at the chain is shown in the last two patterns of her book: a bunch of grapes, which is a piece of free-style tatting and later described under this heading, illustrated in Plate IIIf. For the moment it is sufficient to say that here she has perfected the method of the continuous thread, as she commences the work one yard from the end (the end carrying the sewing needle) and so provides herself with the second thread required for the chain, without a join. She has further developed 'off-shoots' of dead ends, only possible with the false chain. She first makes a little oeillet to neaten the end, and then proceeds with the netting needle to make the stem of the bunch. She says: 'holding the other part of the silk (on the sewing needle) between the 2nd and 3rd fingers, work 9 double stitches'.

At this point Riego had in her hands conditions for making a true chain, i.e. two threads, both of infinite length. The second thread was not fixed, as in the edging described above: it was free, and therefore could be turned to form the stitches. It is a tense moment for the historian who must decide whether or not this is the birth of the chain proper. From the appearance and wording it is impossible to judge: she does not say 'work 9 overcast stitches', which she has said hitherto: she says '*double stitches*' which means correct right and left turns. On the other hand she does not actually state that the second thread has to make the knot. On the whole it seems that the discovery was again postponed – Riego failed by the turn of a thread to realize that she had the means of the discovery of the century in her fingers, and she let it slip from them.

Further attempts: the mandarin sleeve

As in the case of joining by picot, other workers were simultaneously engaged on the search for the chain, and in the following year, 1851, there appeared from another quarter a pattern giving a chain, but again a 'false' one, similar to Riego's. It shows both English and French influence. This time the stitch is called 'a buttonhole stitch' (not overcast) but since it carried picots it was not the buttonhole stitch of today. An anonymous writer for *The Illustrated Exhibitor and Magazine of Art*, a popular periodical of the time, offers a pattern for 'Trimming for a Mandarin Sleeve in *Frivolité*', which appears on a page entitled 'The Ladies' Department'. The pattern consists of directions for making a series of large scallops (in the engraving each scallop measures 4½ inches in width, and 3¾ inches in depth). The scallop consists of five so-called 'leaves', each a group of seven 'ovals' (rings), the groups surrounding a central star-shaped circle. This circle is called a wheel, but it is not the wheel which was evolved later and described as a classic formation. Compared with Riego's patterns, the description is not written with her characteristic accuracy: picots in the illustration are missing in the script. Here again the continuous thread is employed, the first oval beginning about a yard from the end of the thread carrying a sewing needle. A false chain is worked to connect the ovals into their group. The needle thread forms the buttonhole stitches, which lie on the shuttle thread exactly as Riego described in her pattern. A few stitches are worked on the thread between each ring, allowing the group to form a leaf-like shape instead of a circle, which it otherwise would. At the conclusion of the leaf, the chain is continued until a position is reached for starting the next, which is similar. A completed leaf, and four ovals with connecting chains, bearing small picots, i.e. part of the second leaf, is shown in Plate IIIg.

Short bars of 'buttonhole stitch' (similar to the brides in lace-making) connect the leaves to the centrally placed star, worked from and to appropriately placed picots. The whole series of scallops is connected, also by short bars, to one long supporting foundation, or 'heading', also a 'buttonholed' thread. The heading, the star, and the groups of leaves are all laid into position on paper and the bars then worked to shape the piece and connect the whole, as in the French method. Incidentally, the joining by picot is in the modern manner: either this writer worked it out for herself, or had seen 'a Lady's' publication in the same year. This periodical, the *Illustrated Exhibitor*, was connected with the same house which had published the *Ladies' Handbooks* already mentioned. In 1852 there appeared a large cloth-bound volume, *The Ladies' Workbook*, containing many patterns, mostly of crochet, but one of *Frivolité* – the above-mentioned mandarin sleeve trimming.

Again the conditions for making a true tatted chain, i.e. two free threads, were present, and again the opportunity was lost. Several years elapsed before anything else appeared in print, and it seems that efforts towards a final solution were relaxed, and interest flagged. The false chain did what it was meant to do, i.e. connect one part of the pattern to another, and for the moment that was good enough. After all, a straight line could always be provided by crochet, which it frequently was. The fact that a chain would (and did eventually) compose the entire design, had not yet figured in anyone's imagination.

Riego published three more books before she mentions the true chain, and these did not appear until the next decade. *Edgings and Insertions*, 1861, was followed by *Golden Stars in Tatting and Crochet* in the same year: *The Exhibition Tatting Book* appeared in 1862. These three books, which are very small, consisting of an average of eight patterns each, show developments in other directions, but still no advance on the chain. The false chain is occasionally used for short lengths: two or three stitches are made between rings to draw them more closely together in a medallion; the word 'overcast' is now replaced by 'tatting stitches'.

The true chain appears in *The Royal Tatting Book*, published in 1864. The directions are so brief, and so little attention is drawn to it, that it is doubtful if the author realized that here indeed she had achieved, or at least, was describing, what the whole tatting world had been waiting for. As yet, she does not give it a name: nevertheless the chain is a true one, and its description leaves no doubt as to how it is worked. It occurs once only, in a modest little pattern 'Narrow Edging', shown in Plate IIIh.

Narrow edging consists of a neat compact row of scallops, at first sight somewhat resembling the scalloped edging previously described (Plate IIIe), but in construction quite different. The long straight heading of false chain has been replaced by short sections of the true chain, and each scallop is completed before the next is begun.

Six rings of four different sizes are connected by five short chains to make one scallop. The two smallest rings are equal in size and lie on the opposite side of the thread from the larger rings. They are joined head to head and lie along the upper edge of the work. In this pattern, the shuttles are described as 'Red' and 'White', their threads being joined with a knot at the beginning.

After making the first *oeillet* with the white shuttle, she says:

'Turn this oeillet down under the left thumb. The stitches between the oeillets are now worked, using the other thread instead of commencing a loop, thus – place the thread from the red shuttle between the second and third fingers of the left hand, holding it about two inches from the work, and work six double stitches on this thread, so that the white shuttle will form the foundation or drawing thread, and the other the six stitches.'

There is no doubt this time as to the function of each thread. It is the true chain, and moreover, a chain carrying rings on both sides, worked in the correct manner. For here she is also demonstrating one of the advantages of two shuttles: both can make rings – which the second thread attached to a ball can not – and therefore rings can stand on either side of the chain without crossing the threads. All sections of the chain can therefore face in the same direction, while the rings do not. (Cf. Fig. 64.)

Since the chain is of such importance, and the major development of the century, its description as it occurs in *The Complete Tatting Book*, 1865 (first edition), is repeated in full. Riego calls it 'A straight Thread', which is as good a name as any: the word chain is modern, and not a very successful choice. A chain is essentially composed of links, or interlaced rings, and thus is a correct description of one worked in crochet. The French and German words, meaning 'festoon' and 'arch' respectively, are really more suitable.

'"A straight Thread" is instead of commencing a loop, and is used to connect various parts of the pattern together: two threads are always required, with a shuttle for each, or sometimes one end is left attached to the reel: if only a yard or two of cotton is left, the end may be threaded with a sewing needle. The easiest method to describe this will be to fill a red and white shuttle, knotting the two ends of cotton together: hold the knot between the finger and thumb of the left hand, and the thread attached to the red shuttle between the 2nd and 3rd fingers of the same hand, about two inches from the knot: this space of thread is used instead of making a loop: then with the white shuttle in the right hand make a single stitch, pass it up to the knot, keeping the right hand tight: the stitch will be formed by the space of thread, as it would be by a loop: the white shuttle will now be the lower straight thread in the section.'

One may perhaps assume that Riego was the first inventor of the chain, although she does not actually say so. But when in her paragraph on knotting, which she wrote in *The Complete Tatting Book*, she describes the use of knotting – 'to attach that work together when it was made in little pieces, but which my improvements have rendered unnecessary' – she may have been referring to the chain, for it did just that: it joined one ring (or collection of rings) to another.

Since she describes it so carefully, giving a shorter version in *The Lace Tatting Book*, 1866, till finally the description becomes simply a definition in her later publications, it would seem that the honour might be awarded to her. One would feel, with so many imaginative books to her credit, and very probably the false chain, that she deserved it.

The year 1864 had therefore carried tatting to a point in construction which immeasurably broadened the field. It only remained for designers to apply the discovery in the production of patterns which could exploit it to the full.

It is disappointing to record that progress was slow during the ensuing years. There was no one to take immediate advantage of the discovery. A number of workers in fact preferred the ring alone, and some still do: the result is more flexible and delicate. But however reluctantly the chain may have been accepted by a few, the very great advantage it afforded must have been evident to the majority. It must have seemed as if the bond of the ring had been broken (which quite literally it had) and a new freedom – paradoxically acquired by chains – gained. Ability to extend in all directions meant that any shape could be produced, and cutting and joining of threads reduced to a minimum. The chain was generally used in combination with rings; but it can produce some good designs by itself, as modern designers, especially Italian, are discovering. The following examples of the use of the chain, and what it can do, are not necessarily in order of historical development; the simplest are described first, some of which are entirely modern.

NOTE

In all models beginning with the chain, the continuous thread method is used (an unbroken thread on two shuttles) so that there are no free ends at the start.

CHAPTER VI

The Chain

THE chain is capable of variation as it stands: the use of a locking stitch (described under the Knot), differences in tension, working with alternate shuttles, and reversing the work, alter its length and direction. Its various forms are shown in Figures 45–55 on Plate V.

The simplest shape of the chain is a straight line, in which case the tension of the running thread is such that the threads on its upper edge have room to lie straight. If the running thread is pulled more tightly, the extra threads will cause the line to be drawn into a curve, as there are more threads on the upper edge than on the lower. In most modern patterns the chain is curved.

If pulled very tightly it curves round on itself, holding its shape as a flat spiral. The tension is slackened as the curve flattens.

If the tension varies at different places, and the work is reversed at intervals, the curve will become external instead of internal, and vice versa. The stitches on the running thread always lie on the outside of the curve, i.e. face outwards. The example holds itself, but appropriate picots would keep it more rigid.

After a straight section, a locking stitch is made to break the tension: the work is reversed, and there follows a sharply curved section: another locking stitch, and the sequence is repeated. Almost any outline could be 'drawn' in this manner.

If the shuttles are alternated at regular intervals, and sections pulled up tightly, a row of scallops results. The same scallopped effect would be achieved by making a locking stitch after each section without alternating the shuttles.

If the chain (tightly worked) is reversed at intervals, it produces scallops facing both ways (internal and external curves), without alternating the shuttles. (The double scallop.)

If the chain is made of all single stitches, a rigid corkscrew twist results.

Picots on the chain

Chains (Figs. 45–50 inclusive) can carry picots including one at the beginning or head (of practical value in free-style work). The picots may be any length and any distance apart.

If picots are carried by Figure 46 (the flat spiral) it can link on to itself as it grows, to form a solid mat.

Picots may lie on both sides of the chain. The work is reversed immediately after the picot is made.

On a double scallop (as in Fig. 55) measured graduated picots produce a feathered effect. This is a development of the preceding figure: the chain is reversed after a series of picots instead of after a single one.

The mock-ring (Figs. 56–58, Plate V)

A title has so far not been applied to this formation, which has recently been revived and is now in frequent use.

A chain may qualify for the title of mock-ring when it is made to appear like a closed ring by bringing the end round to the beginning, or very near it. The two ends may be linked into a picot (or picots) on the main fabric, or the picot may be made at the beginning of the mock-ring itself, as shown in the example. Formed in this way, a mock-ring can be the centre of a medallion.

In Figure 57 the picots are purposely wider apart to show the passage of the chain, but near enough to describe it as a mock-ring. A central ring carrying six picots (two sizes alternately placed) has been made. Following on with the same threads, a chain is worked, linking into the small picots. If carried right round the result would be three 'mock-rings', forming a medallion somewhat resembling flower petals.

Although we have not quite reached the ring and chain in combination, as we are still dealing only with chains, rings must here be mentioned in connection with the mock-ring. One of the principal reasons for the mock-ring is its ability to carry ornamental rings upon itself, which the real ring cannot do. These (usually Josephine rosettes) are made by the second shuttle and are literally carried by the mock-ring, which supports them. It is not an arrangement of rings alternating with chains, a combination shown later. The passage of the running thread is not interrupted throughout its length, and therefore it is one chain from beginning to end. Such a distinction is necessary for the accurate description of patterns. A nearly enclosed mock-ring is shown carrying three rosettes, and the beginning of a second.

The mock-ring has a number of applications, more of which will be described later. It is one of the important features to recognize when observing the construction of a piece.

DESIGNS COMPOSED OF CHAINS ALONE (Figs. 59–61, Plate VI)

Edgings

A number of edgings can be made from chains alone, the simplest being one round of Figure 49, which can consist of as few as three double stitches for each scallop. If larger, it can carry a central picot to which another round may be attached. After the first row of scallops has been made, and sewn to the material it is to trim, it is not necessary to alternate the shuttle again as the ensuing rounds will follow the curve. The number of decorative picots is of course optional. The example shows three rounds, every scallop consisting of sixteen doubles.

This lively Italian edging is a break-away from tradition with its solid cubes: it is worked in one round.

Medallions

This medallion, derived from a modern German design, is a relief from the usual ornament. The only picots are purely functional and very small. The centre is a mock-ring, carrying eight picots. The next round follows immediately with the same pair of threads; it is a simple chain linking into picots on the mock-ring and carrying very small picots in the centre of each section. The following rounds are all worked on independent pairs of threads, connecting with the picots on the previous rounds.

Since chains have the faculty of imitating rings, they can in effect do everything that rings do, and more, besides forming motifs of which they alone are capable. They compose the principal formations of free-style work, since they have complete versatility and are able to lend themselves more easily to the use of multiple threads, especially threads of different type and calibre, which cannot be so successfully manipulated on the ring. On such occasions a mock-ring answers the purpose.

CHAPTER VII

The Ring and Chain in combination

COMBINATIONS of rings and chains, whether in edgings, medallions, or virtually any shape, are unlimited. It is impossible to do more than indicate a few ways in which they can be built together (Figs. 62–64, Plate VI).

The scroll and its variations

The simplest ring and chain unit is one universally used: it gives a scroll-like effect, and although it has no particular name it can be considered as a classical formation. It consists simply of a row of rings (of any size) connected by, or alternating with chains, which can be any length, but a good proportion is one where the number of stitches in both is equal. As it stands, it can be used as a simple one-round edging. Here the ring and chain are of equal importance, one following the other, i.e. alternating.

If the *shuttles* are alternated between the rings and chains, the latter can remain straight (instead of curved), the running thread being independent of the rings and acting as a drawstring for the entire length. This can be used as a means of regulating the tension right round a circle. Here the rings are being carried by the (one) chain, in the same manner as the mock-ring carries the Josephine rosettes.

Rings can be placed on both sides of a chain. The second shuttle makes the rings which lie on the upper side of the chain, in order to avoid the crossing of threads: the first shuttle makes the lower rings, and therefore the running line is interrupted at this point.

Lines into areas

Following the sequence of lines into areas, if Figure 62 is pulled round into a circle, the conclusion is a simple medallion whose centre is an enclosed space: this time the rings face inwards (Fig. 65, Plate VII).

Since the medallion is a recognized form, i.e. a complete design with a limiting outline to define its shape (usually circular, square, or oval) an attempt has been made to classify it, based on its construction. The classification includes those made of both ring and chain, or either one.

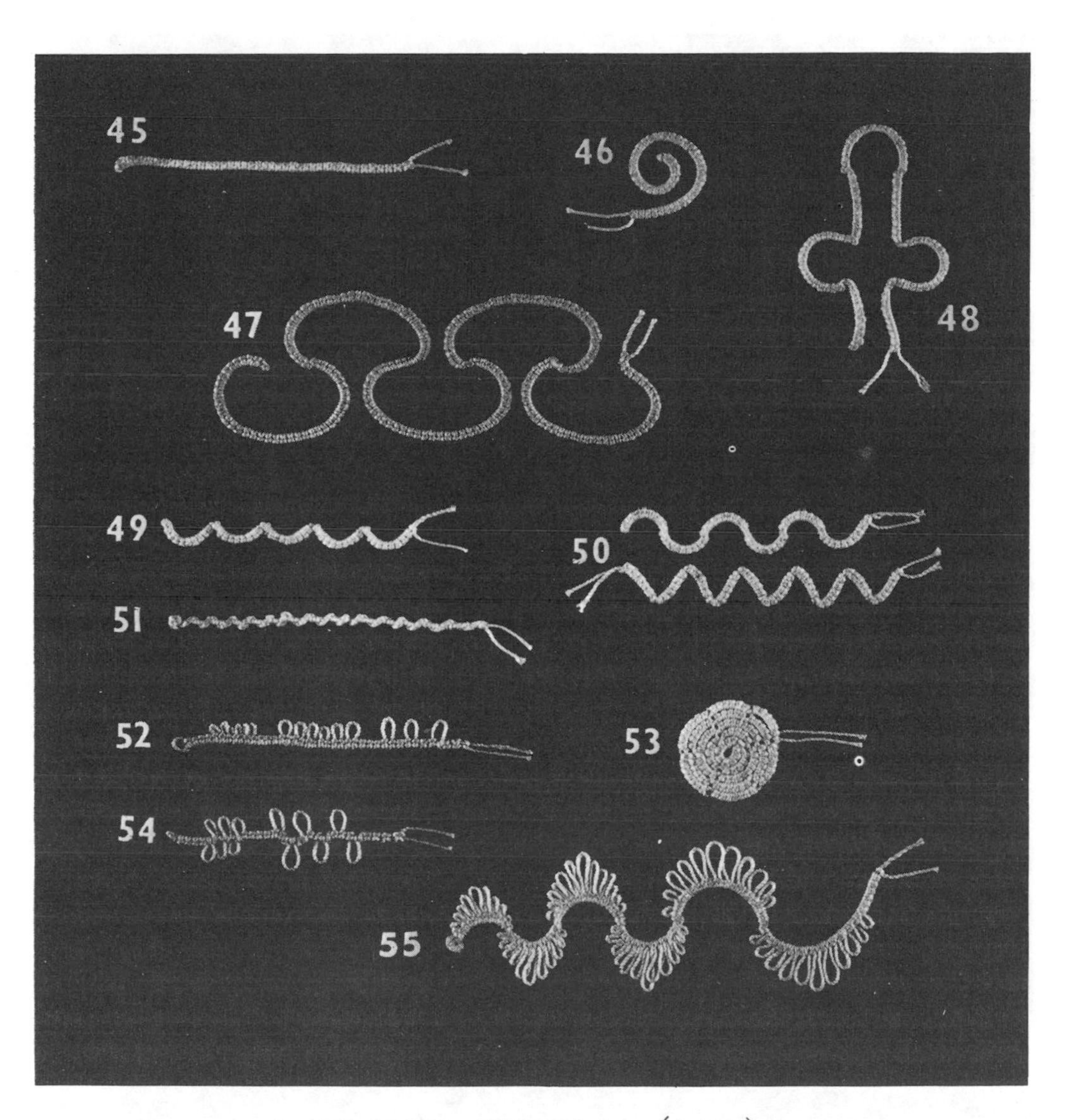

THE CHAIN · FIGURES 45–50 (*page* 44)

THE CHAIN WITH PICOTS · FIGURES 51–55 (*page* 45)

THE MOCK-RING · FIGURES 56–58 (*page* 45)

PLATE V

DESIGNS COMPOSED OF CHAINS ALONE · FIGURES 59–61 (*page* 46)

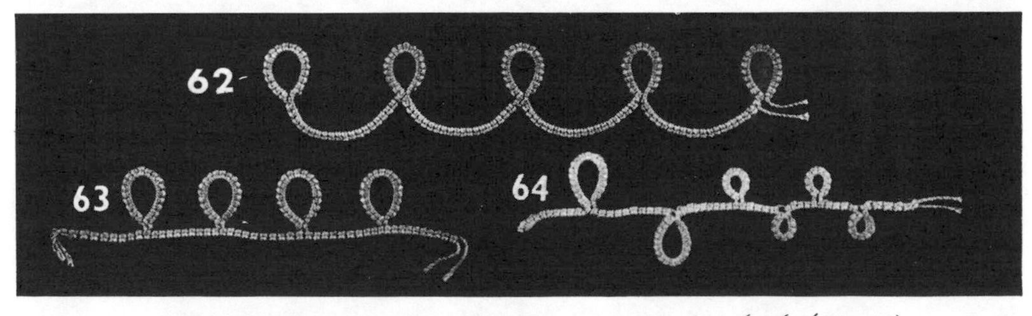

COMBINATIONS OF RING AND CHAIN · FIGURES 62–64 (*page* 47)

PLATE VI

CHAPTER VIII

Medallions and Pattern Repetition

BROADLY speaking the medallion can be classified into three groups, according to the nature of its centre. The centre may consist of a single ring (or mock-ring): an enclosed space: or a large picot. No definition is completely clear-cut, however, and other groups no doubt await discovery (Plate VII).

The central ring group

This group includes the daisy and the wheel (Figs. 42 and 43), consisting of a central ring bearing picots to which the ensuing round may be attached.

The enclosed space group

This group includes the oldest forms. If we look back to the original basic shapes we see that three or more rings may be drawn together forming an enclosed space (albeit sometimes a very small one). This enclosure forms the heart of a trefoil, quatrefoil, cinquefoil, etc. to which new rounds may be attached. An example built on to a trefoil (which gives the minimum space) is shown in Figure 66. The space is so small that the trefoil gives the appearance of a solid centre, nevertheless it belongs to the enclosed space group. The round following it is simply the scroll (Fig. 62) with three of the chains slightly longer than the others.

Chains, too, can form an enclosed space: an example is shown under the square medallion, described later.

In the original basic shapes, composed of rings alone, the rings faced outwards. Joined by a chain they can face inwards, i.e. they are inverted. Figure 65 previously described shows ten rings and chains drawn into a circle, but there can be any number: strengthened with chains they can set the shape of the medallion, not necessarily circular.

The central picot group (Figs. 67–69, Plate VII)

Where the rings face inwards, they may be so closely set that it is an advantage to join them together, all at one point, i.e. head to head. The ring first made carries a long picot at its apex: all the other rings link into it. Such an arrangement can no longer be described as rings enclosing a space, as the space is now occupied by a picot. Therefore this formation belongs to an independent group, although closely related to the one before it. The example shows an inverted cinquefoil, the rings linked in this manner. (This longer picot is often used to hold two or more rings together – not necessarily in a medallion.)

A further and unusual example is this all-ring medallion, composed of Figure 15 (rings on both sides of the thread). The first inner ring made carries a very large picot into which all the other (inner) rings are linked: if correctly worked the picot is not apparent. It is an ingenious arrangement as it manages to make the rings face inwards without the assistance of a chain, besides holding them firmly together in a circle. This particular example is de Dillmont's nearest approach to the wheel and is of historical interest. A central ring would now replace the large picot, thus producing the wheel, of which this example is a near relation.

A chain also can carry a long picot (either at the beginning or farther along its course) which lies at the centre. In the example shown, the picot is formed after a short section of chain (one side of one of the 'spokes') has been worked. The chain is worked back and forth from the circumference to this picot, with which it engages every time the centre is reached. When the chain is at the circumference it carries a clover (Fig. 41) and then returns to the centre, lying closely to the last section: after linking into the central picot it begins the next spoke. The whole is worked as one round, on one pair of threads.

The central picot group is the most interesting one, as the picot may or may not be apparent, and it is often hard to detect its presence. It is not easy to make, because if it is too small, there will not be room for all the motifs to link into it, and if too large the intended shape of the medallion (circular, oval, etc.) will be lost; besides which the whole proportion of the piece is thrown out and the succeeding round will not fit on to the first one. The exact size of the picot can only be arrived at by trial and error. If a large number of rings or chains (sometimes sixteen) are used, the picot will have to be so large that it gives the impression of an enclosed space. We have therefore a second paradox: firstly the trefoil appeared to give a solid centre, whereas it really encloses a space: and here a central picot, beyond a certain size, gives the opposite impression to its true construction.

The square medallion

The square medallion is often used in furnishing as it is particularly suited to the decoration of square and rectangular tablecloths, place mats, pillowcases, and of course handkerchiefs, in which they can appear as a border or insertion. They are quite as interesting to work as the circle, and a number can be laid side by side, or corner to corner, diamond-wise. A true diamond (or rhombus) is a squashed square: instead of its angles being equal, two are sharper and two are flatter, but the principle of working it is the same. (Given the same length of side as the square, the diamond covers less area.) Classification of squares is the same as for the circle.

The square from rings alone (Figs. 70–71, Plate VII)

A primitive square can be made from two parallel rows of rings, equally spaced on the threads, pairs of rings in one row joining with their opposite in the row above them. They are united by a centre picot carried on the ring made first.

An all-ring square can be developed from the original basic shape (Fig. 17) by adding four smaller rings to give it a more defined body. (Enclosed space group.) Other rounds may be added, preserving its shape.

The square from rings and chains (Figs. 72–75, Plate VII)

The scroll, of four rings, united high on the shoulders instead of at the sides, joined by longer chains, gives a neat square with rounded corners. This is much used in modern patterns, not necessarily in medallions. The rings could equally well be joined by a central picot (as in the inverted cinquefoil, Fig. 67).

The scroll of eight rings, with the corner chains longer than the others, gives a larger, rigid square with well-defined lines.

These are the simplest possible examples. A more elaborate one, worked in finer thread, is from a Spanish design. It is composed of four clovers, facing outwards, joined to one another by chains, which form an enclosed centre space: the round following it is again the scroll, as in the previous figure, but instead of enlarging the corners the rings are orientated to form a pronounced right-angle.

The problem of designing a square from motifs composing an edging may occur in handkerchief borders. A square results naturally when two straight bands of edging meet at right-angles, i.e. at the corners, which are the most important part of the design. The pattern shown in the border must be preserved as far as possible:

a new motif should not be introduced. Examples of handkerchief edgings and corners are shown in the practical section.

The diamond illustrated is modern Italian and like the preceding figure, the Spanish square, it is also composed of clovers; but this time they face inwards (also forming an enclosed centre space). There are six, to accommodate the elongated diamond shape, and they are joined by picots very near to their tips. The clovers are connected, not by the scroll, but by a simple chain. The result is a hexagon, to which is added (on new threads) a clover to two opposite sides, to make the acute angles.

Both these figures are good examples of building basic shapes from the simplest of motifs: the clover lends itself particularly well as it is a triangular shape, and we have seen how versatile the triangle can be in building simple geometrical forms.

Pattern repetition

In the patterns, the word 'repetition' signifies a collection of motifs, whether one ring or a complicated formation, which are repeated in the same order. But it also has a wider meaning. The repetition of a *design* is one complete collection, which, when identically repeated for the required number of times, produces the finished shape. As such, it is a theoretical division: its boundaries can be assumed at any two points in the design. It does not necessarily coincide with the manner or order of work, as for instance in the case of a medallion built round a central ring: each complete repetition will include a fraction of the ring. It does coincide in a one-round edging and in medallions which are worked to and from the centre.

The number of repetitions should always be noted in a medallion. Any number is theoretically possible, but four, six, eight and twelve are the most common. A square (and diamond) will always consist of four repetitions, each being a quarter of the whole figure.

In a diamond, two repetitions will be the mirror image of the other two. Three, five and seven are now coming into favour, especially five. The number has a practical consequence for the worker. They may appear very distinctly, as separate divisions, or be only slightly indicated. Where they are frequent, and not very pronounced, it does not matter how the medallion is placed in relation to another of the same design. They will look identical. If, however, the repetition occurs only a few times the pattern will not appear the same unless they are placed the same way up, i.e. all must show the repetitions in the same position relative to the background. The effect of an ill-balanced medallion is obvious, as shown in Figure 76.

The repetition in patterns of edgings applied to a fabric of a given length is of great practical importance and is discussed in Part 2, under handkerchief borders.

Brief description of plates

Plates VIII to *X* inclusive give examples of medallions, many of which are worked from foreign pattern books. They illustrate compositions already described, and also some that are more advanced. All three types, the Central Ring, Enclosed Space, and Central Picot, are represented: they provide a useful exercise in observation as to their construction.

Plate VIII shows medallions of five repetitions: one represents the White Rose of York, and contains an advanced arrangement of the picot which fills the petals. Figure 53 (the flat spiral) is applied to the centre after it is worked: it has been slightly modified and carries many small picots. The two small five-petalled flowers are described in my book *A New Look in Tatting*, which deals exclusively with flower construction.

Plate IX shows medallions of three, six and twelve repetitions: two were inspired by a marble mosaic; these show the repetitions very strongly.

Plate X: A piece of tatted fabric, mounted on net, composed of six-sided (or six-armed) medallions. The medallion, which is from de Dillmont, is composed of four of the figures previously described, thus:

1st round Figure 19 forms the inner circle, or main part. (Six rings giving an enclosed space centre.)

2nd round A chain is worked right round the inner circle, joining to it at its picots. Where one ring joins its neighbour, a Josephine rosette (Fig. 13) is worked on the second shuttle. At the apex of each ring the chain forms a mock-ring, joining into the picot before and after. The mock-ring carries three picots, the centre one for engagement with a corresponding picot on a neighbouring medallion (Fig. 35).

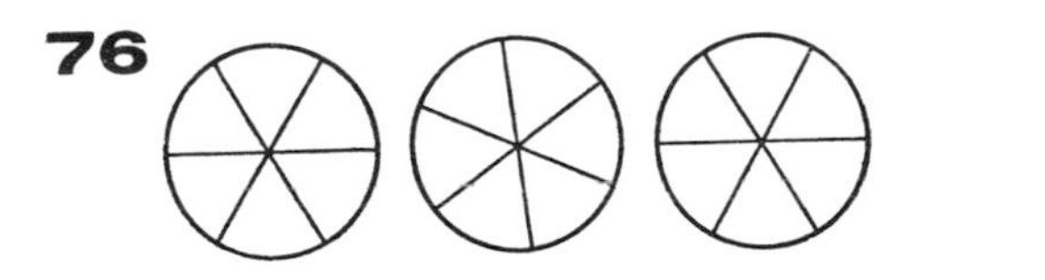

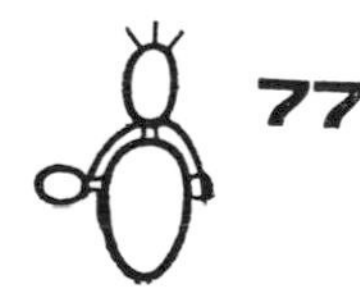

The repetition for the medallion is shown in Figure 77.
The repetition for the entire fabric is one medallion.

Heart-shaped forms

These include three specimen pieces: The Daisy Chain, Rococo Rose, and a Tudor Rose.

Shapes that cannot be worked by 'rounds', either concentric, or to and from the centre, are composed of independently worked motifs, joined to one another in a specified order. These three examples were constructed in this manner. They are intended to show how compositions may be built up into an unusual shape, in formations not usually associated with the more conventional patterns. (Illustrated in Plates XI, XII, and XIII).

Plate XI: Shaped bands of massed picots form the five inner petals of the Tudor Rose. The centre is a modified version of Figure 53. See description of the Rose of York, in Plate VIII.

Plate XII: Rococo Rose. A large centrally placed medallion is connected to two smaller ones at the shoulders of the heart by Figure 55 (graduated picots on both sides of a chain). These chains form double intersections (Fig. 95) with a small mock-ring. Sprays of tiny flowers and leaves form the sides which connect with a smaller medallion at the base.

Plate XIII: The Daisy Chain. So called on account of the rows of small picot-bearing rings, which it features. (Not related to the classic Daisy.) Small flower-like motifs are assembled to form the whole, which is surrounded by a single chain, starting from and ending at a clover.

CHAPTER IX

Free-style Tatting

FREE-STYLE tatting is a modern name for individually worked pieces which represent a selected natural form – usually a flower or a spray. The fact that a stylized form of flowers and leaves is suggested by simple tatting formations has long been recognized, and practised by certain workers.

In Riego's earliest book of 1850 there is a pattern for an 'Appliqué Waistcoat'. This magnificent piece of male apparel is decorated with 106 bunches of grapes, worked in coloured shaded silks. The bunches are sewn on to the waistcoat, and connected by a crochet chain – a 'soutache' of gold twist and green silk, bearing additional tendrils of gold. Constant reference to this piece has been made throughout this book, as it combines (in a remarkably small compass) so many distinctive features and represents the epitome of evolution for that year. Since it is of great historical interest, being the first recorded example of free style, a brief but comprehensive review of its features are given once again.

1. It is worked with needles, which indicate the date.
2. It is constructed with coloured silks and gold thread.
3. It is worked on a continuous thread.
4. The shuttle thread loops back on itself to form a false chain, to provide the leaf stalks, thus forming off-shoots from the main stem, or 'dead ends'.
5. The thread passes behind the rings and is forced through the worked line to bring it into position for the next row.

The pattern for the bunch of grapes was followed exactly, using cotton No. 20 and two darning needles, and is shown in Plate IIIf. Riego also used this motif as decoration for 'a Mourning Collar', described in Chapter X.

Lady Hoare used many natural forms as models, which she introduced into her work. She made many groups of what she described as 'roses, grapes in clusters, vine-leaves with tendrils, lilies'. These were usually arranged as trailing sprays, requiring support to hold them in position, so were mounted on net. Some of these arrangements were composed entirely of rings, a string of elongated half-rings connecting the groups of flowers. An insertion composed of acorns and pomegranates was made of thicker thread, so that it held its shape. The acorn is an oval ring, the interior filled with a small piece of fine-meshed net: it is closely surrounded by a mock-ring. The pomegranates are large clusters or bunches of overlapping small rings, giving the appearance of seeds.

A number of unusual formations were made possible by her inspired use of the chain, since she reversed it to produce alternating curves, made it carry picots on both sides, formed the double scallop, and applied the mock-ring.

Modern Italian patterns have recently shown a tendency towards flower-forms, incorporated in simple designs. An original pattern for Queen Anne's Lace (one of the varieties of Cow Parsley), and intended for mounting on a foundation as a picture, is given in Part 2.

THE ALPHABET AND ARITHMETICAL FIGURES (Figs. 78–81, Plate XIV)

Some royal examples: Queen Marie used, and probably originated, several styles of lettering appropriate to the article which carried it, according to its domestic or ecclesiastical environment. One of her finest pieces is a baby's coverlet of tatting with some embroidery stitches. Seventeen large capital letters of the Greek alphabet are arranged to form a circle: the letters are built up of three parallel rows of a plain chain, the few cross bars that exist are made separately and lie beneath them. Each letter rests on an oval worked shape (tatting?) of a honeycomb appearance, which throws it up in relief. Outside the circle, spaced round the coverlet, which is square, are six words composed in 'script' tatting, each word formed from one continuous chain, overlapping upon itself where the letters require it. There are therefore no breaks or joins between the letters.

A very large letter (a capital J), presumably part of a ceremonial piece, is of a different type. Its illustration, which is life size, measures 8½ inches in height, 1½ inches across the shaft, and an overall width of 4½ inches. Two parallel bands of Figure 47 form the letter, including the upper and lower strokes, which are worked in one with the shaft, so no applied pieces are necessary. Here the motif is reduced in size to accommodate the curves. The bands are joined by a chain, continuous throughout,

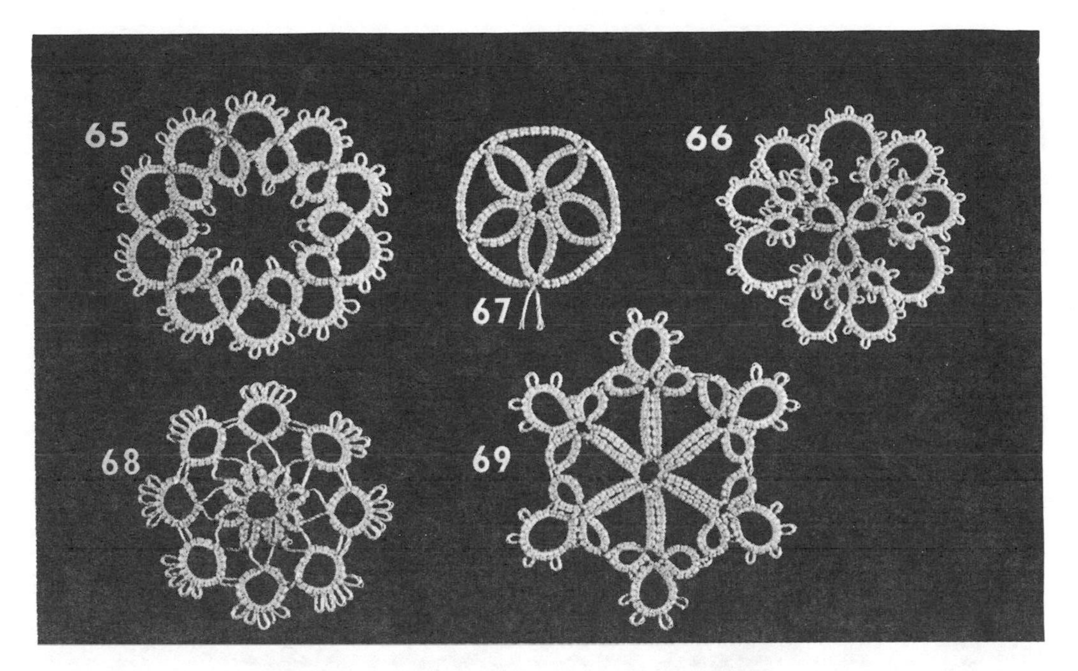

PLATE VII THE MEDALLION · FIGURES 65–75 (*pages* 49–52)

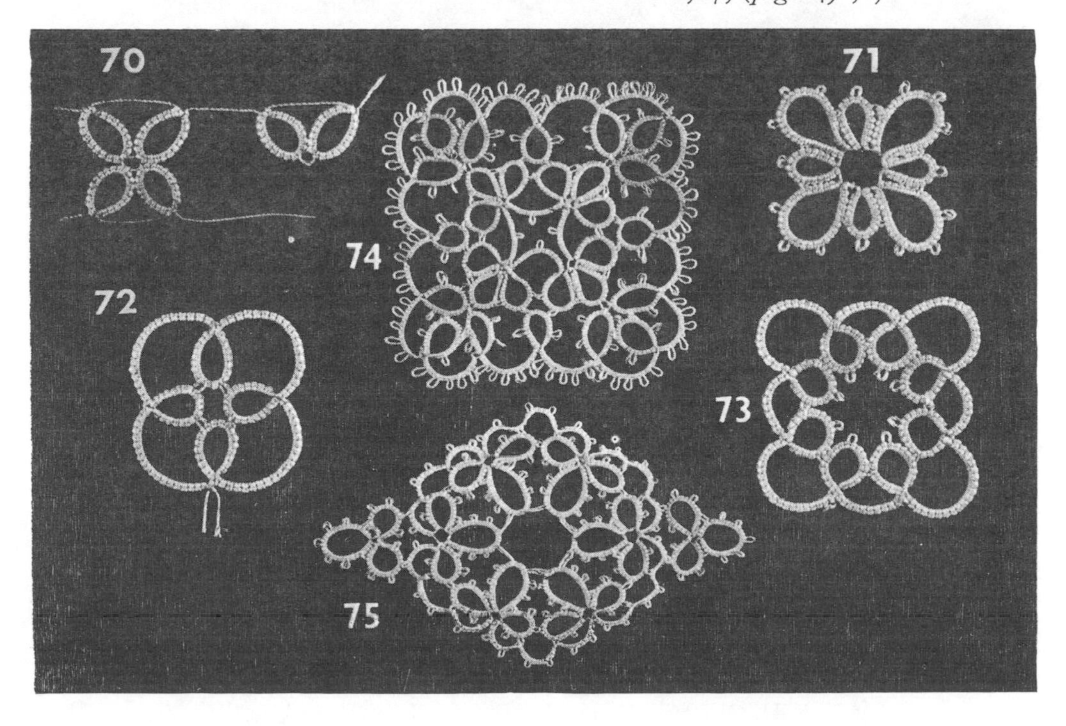

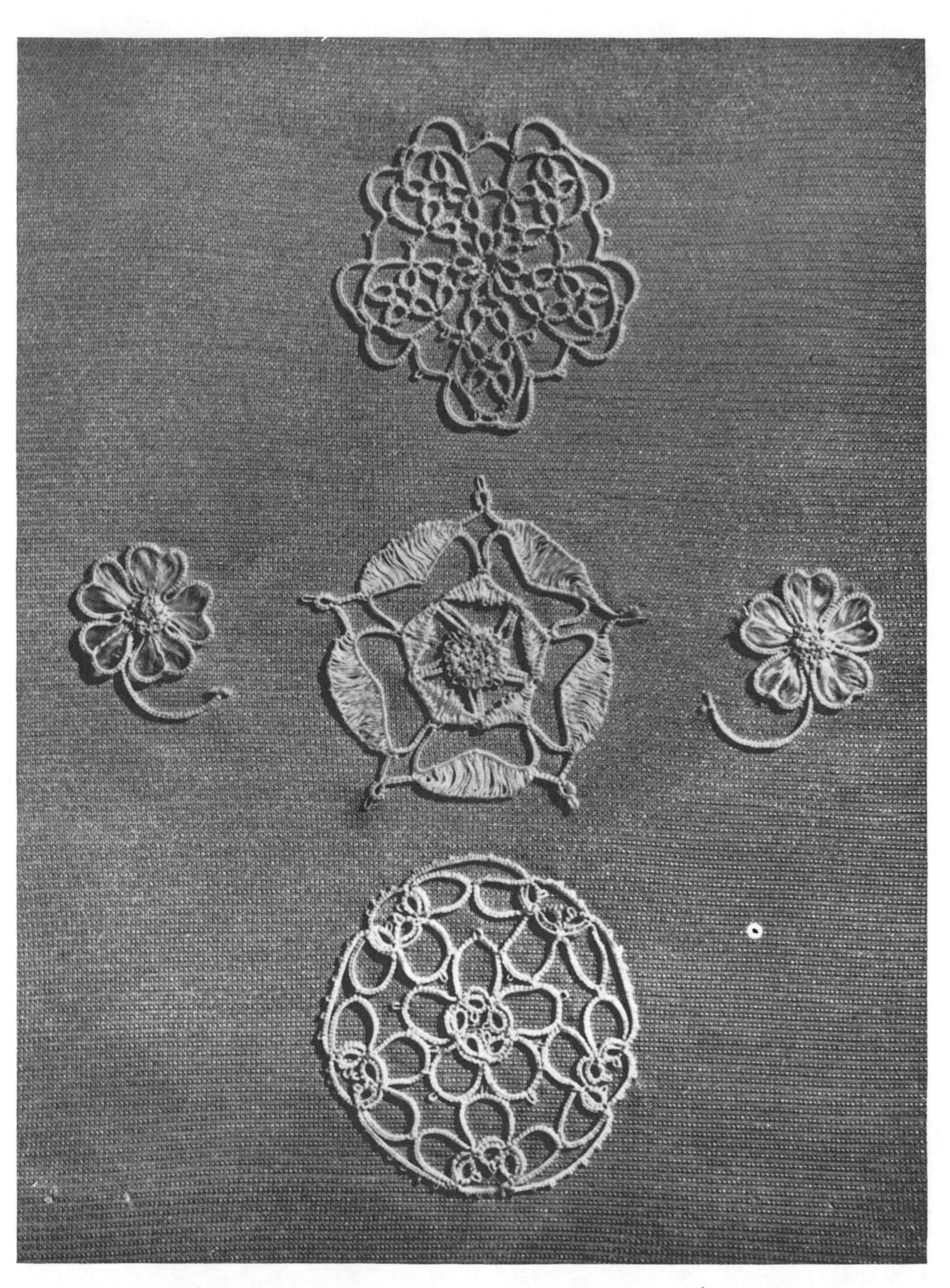

PLATE VIII MEDALLIONS OF FIVE REPETITIONS (*page* 53)

PLATE IX MEDALLIONS OF THREE, SIX, AND TWELVE REPETITIONS (*page* 53)

PLATE X TATTED FABRIC MOUNTED ON NET (six-sided medallions) (*page* 53)

and they are bordered by two parallel rows of chains, heavily picoted: these form the border of the letter. The whole is worked in gold thread on a silk running thread. In large examples of this kind, there is room for almost any composition which lends itself to repetition without an undue number of joins, and which can be reduced to form curves and angles of appropriate proportions.

Styles of lettering

Several attempts have been made by modern designers to produce alphabets, but tatting is not really suitable as a medium for this purpose. In the first place, tatting should look like itself. Being essentially composed of curves, it abhors a straight line: to force it into one for more than a short distance is to imitate a shape that is foreign to its real nature. The final effect is one of falseness. As an illustration of this, an example is given of Roman characters, which were originally designed for excision in stone. Fine proportions, thick and thin strokes and ornamental serifs are a feature of Roman lettering: tatting cannot successfully reproduce these. The example is composed of carefully proportioned unornamented strokes, and while it gives a not unpleasant effect it is at best an imitation and is not a true expression of the medium.

Letters are perhaps justified when used as monograms or single initials, when they can be large enough to display the distinctive feature of the work, and applied ornament would not be out of character. Figure 79 shows an example where the natural curve of the chain has been exploited without ornament, but they cannot hold their essential shape and must be sewn into position on to a background.

Three fancy letters, a capital O, N and T in different styles are shown, chosen because each displays its particular feature to advantage. In single letters such as these, which are isolated examples, profuse ornament is not out of place. The T combines a reversing chain with a ring; the N displays a corkscrew twist; in the O, which is worked all on one pair of threads, pairs of picots lie across one another. These features would not be so successful in many of the other letters of the alphabet.

Three letters are shown here which are based on a free modification of a very old alphabet, in which the principal straight lines have been deliberately translated into curves. The letters are composed of pairs of chains lying closely together, of correct tension for the amount of curvature they need to indicate. The curves are relieved by a small ornamental ring at their junctions. These letters will hold their shape if the tension is well balanced, and the theme is possible in all twenty-six characters.

Two signatures and a date, worked as a continuous chain, complete the page.

CHAPTER X

Other Materials used with Tatting

Net foundation

CERTAIN kinds of real lace, notably Brussels, is worked on to a net foundation with a needle, both materials constituting the completed lace. Tatting can also be applied to net, but it is worked separately and the pieces sewn on. The net therefore is not strictly part of the tatting. However, the net provides part of the whole design, since in any drawing composed of lines, the shape of the spaces they enclose is as important as the lines themselves. The net allows decorative spaces to exist between unjoined motifs: very small ones can be scattered over its surface. Net therefore might be considered as an accessory part of the whole.

Riego used material for making 'a mourning collar' which appears in her book of 1850. She decorates it with her bunches of grapes, which, she says, 'are made in fine black tatting silk, or Shetland wool, for mounting on cambric, crape, or white brussels net'.

Dillmont's book (1924) shows four examples: strips of tulle carry highly ornamental edgings of several rounds. The edge of the tulle has been previously cut into vandykes, oversewn with the tatting thread. All the models are scattered with varieties of tiny rings and knots for several inches in depth. When it is realized that every knot has to be sewn on separately, and has two ends of thread which must not show, the amount of time and patience spent on such work can scarcely be estimated.

Lady Hoare used nets of varying sized meshes – some very fine, both black and white. She called the result 'appliqué work' and made complete articles: caps, scarves, collars, and also smaller pieces of trimming. The edge of the net, like Dillmont's, was often scalloped to accommodate the tatted motifs. Photographs in her book show pieces of great delicacy, every one an original specimen, the design produced for the shape of the garment. The Josephine rings, which were sometimes scattered over the surface, she called 'spots' and notes that 'they were put in by hand'. In other words, she was not working on a piece of machine-spotted net.

Tatting with embroidery

Some embroidery, from simple connecting stitches to the more elaborate spider's web, has been used since very early times: the first shapes in tatting as we have seen were circles of rings enclosing a space which needed to be filled in to help hold the rings in place.

Riego shows a pattern of what she describes as Greek Lace Trimming: it is an edging of deep vandykes, and the larger rings composing them are filled with spider's webs; here the ring itself is filled, not a circle of rings. The placing of a web in the centre of a medallion is now being favoured by Italian designers.

Queen Marie frequently made recourse to a needle and thread. She describes a chalice veil in thick white silk, 'and oversewn in places with buttonhole stitch'. In another piece 'little falling tassels were done with the needle'.

Tatting with crochet

Crochet was probably applied to tatting not long after it was introduced, since it provided a straight chain which at that time tatting could not. The first recorded example of its use is in Riego's book of 1850 when it is applied as a decorative trimming: a crocheted chain of gold thread, combined with silk, connects the bunches of grapes which are sewn to a foundation. In her second book, *Edgings and Insertions*, it provides a 'heading' or base, upon which the tatting stands, forming a straight line. In this book the word 'circle' now appears instead of *oeillet* or rosette. Some of the circles are half-rings, i.e. not fully drawn up, and in one case the crochet chain forms stitches on to the 'free' thread of the half-ring, in between the stitches forming the straight heading, which makes the whole much firmer. This was no doubt an advantage in pieces which were made for trimming clothing: together with 'the new method of joining' they were now capable of much harder wear, and frequent washing. An unobtrusive border of a simple crochet chain surrounds medallions described in *Golden Stars in Tatting and Crochet* (1861). In *The Royal Tatting Book* (1864), a crochet chain is used to connect tatted stars to form a medallion, a number of which constitute an antimacassar. The crochet gives the appearance of netting.

Dillmont uses a great deal of crochet in her early books, making crochet 'braids' on to which tatting is sewn, for a border to a bedspread made of medallions in both tatting and crochet. Later, her successor uses a band of crochet to join two edgings of tatting, placed back to back. She also works three rows of crochet as a border for tatted insertions (both sides). Such borders provide a firm solid edging which would be necessary in a fine insertion to prevent it from tearing away. Modern Swedish designers use crochet for the same purpose, on edgings, to provide a firm band for attachment to the edge of material; this is stronger than a fine sewing thread through a picot.

Tatting with beads and precious stones

Riego uses steel and jet beads in a pattern for 'Parisian Gimp Trimming', to be applied to 'paletots, jackets and trimmings', for which she used coarse black Maltese silk. The beads were strung on to the thread of the second shuttle, in the same way that beads are used in knitting; the running thread passes outside the bead. A chain round the outer edges of the trimming carried the beads, placed a short distance apart. They are thus incorporated into the fabric. Short bars of five beads threaded on to the silk in the normal way are sewn in afterwards to connect parts of the pattern together in the manner of 'brides'.

Queen Marie made free use of precious stones and with them ornamented many of her elaborate ecclesiastical pieces. Stones which were pierced were worked into the fabric (as the bead): she describes 'a chalice cover in very fine white silk with real pearls: the silk thread is drawn through the pearls with a hair and then tatted into the work, not put on afterwards'. No description is given as to how the jewels were applied when they were not pierced and could not be worked on directly. Possibly each was held in a gold claw setting which would give purchase for a needle and thread. This form of attachment was probably used for a chalice cover 'with a border of crystal drops'.

The largest, and what must have been one of the Queen's finest pieces, is described in her own words:

'. . . a curtain for the door of the Iconostasis in the Church of Sinaia, two metres long, tatted in yellow brown silk. The Byzantine cross is embroidered over in buttonhole stitch with a topaz in each marguerite. The background . . is embroidered in gold thread in lace stitch, and every marguerite has a turquoise in the middle . . .'

Such magnificence would not be in the present taste and fashion, but as a period piece, indicative of its time and place, it must be unsurpassed.

FOREWORD TO PART 2

FOR THE BEGINNER

IF, on reading the first part of the book, which is for already established workers, you feel sufficiently interested in contributing to the survival of tatting, you should now master the stitch (assuming you have not already done so) and make the shuttle create for you.

It is a rewarding field. Few crafts require so little outlay: the tools and materials are few, and inexpensive. It can be practised at odd moments by almost anyone, anywhere, in trains or in bed. The section to follow describes what you need and how to make easy pieces, which will serve as an introduction to the more elaborate. The few patterns given are described in great detail and are progressive. Working them with understanding will give a knowledge of the craft which will increase with every piece you make. Not everyone needs to work up to exhibition standard: in any case exhibitions and competitions for prizes are not the main objects of an artist. Beautiful things personally created bring the satisfaction an artist seeks, and in this craft, these are within the scope of everybody who has patience and an interest in using her hands.

Every piece made is a proof that the craft still lives and is a contribution to its further development, as well as an expression of individual taste and skill. A craft that is alive adapts itself to new circumstances – the very definition of any form of life. Tatting does just this, as it is adaptable to the current fashion as much as it ever was, whether as Elizabethan ruffle, Victorian antimacassar, or a modern evening bag. The following suggestions are for everyday needs in our own time.

CHAPTER I

Things to Make, Materials and Tools

TATTING can be simply a decoration in itself, applied as an ornament to some other article, or can constitute the article itself. Where it forms ornament only, it must, for contemporary taste, be suitable to its environment. Fifty years ago decoration was produced for its own sake, and was applied to articles in the home with comparative abandon. The Victorian dressing table, for example, was not complete unless it was draped with flounces and the articles upon it, many of them now out of date, were embellished with one form or another of hand-work. An out-size pincushion, watch stand, hairpin and hat-pin cases, and hair-tidy all received lavish trimmings, as did the nightdress case, handkerchief and glove sachets in the dressing table drawer. The modern coiffure and its care has eliminated the need for some of these objects; just as the pen-wiper, blotting book and card case (equally prone to decoration) have disappeared from the writing desk in favour of a Biro pen or a portable typewriter. With the passing of Victorian impedimenta, new ways of applying tatting for personal use have been sought. It still has a place on the modern dressing table, although this is swept comparatively bare and its mats, originally made to lie beneath candlesticks, now frequently lie beneath a sheet of glass. Here they are still decorative, and their decoration does not interfere with function, since they have none. New manners and customs create new products: attractive cases for powder compacts can be made of two medallions joined around three-quarters of the edge, lined with silk.

Things to wear

Edgings and insertions of all kinds, for lingerie: collars or edgings for collars: yokes for blouses and nightdresses: short-sleeved cardigans: trimmings for bed-jackets. A small medallion, spray of stylized flowers or other motif may be pinned to a blouse, coat lapel, or ornamental pocket. Gloves in écru or coloured cotton, entirely of tatting or lightly ornamented with it: small trimmings for hats and hat-veils: bride's coronets and trimmings for veils: narrow edgings for nurses' caps and apron bibs: even fancy earrings have been designed, of two medallions, a smaller applied to a larger and both sewn to a clip.

Things to use

Edgings and insertions can be applied to bedroom and bathroom linen. The top sheet can carry an edging, also the pillow case, either right round or on the two ends only. The average pillow case is nine feet round, so the two ends will probably be sufficient. Face towels can carry a deeper edging, at one end only, but as these require frequent washing, the design should be a firm one that is not easily pulled out of shape.

Evening bags can be made entirely of tatting, and lined: or one of a plain material can be trimmed to match the dress. Also fans: either all of lace, or of material to which motifs can be applied; these must be sufficiently fine to follow the folds of the fan, and must be designed so that the stitches applying them do not coincide with the fan 'sticks'.

Furnishings of the modern dinner table provide more scope than the Victorian, when a large white tablecloth and plain napkins permitted no alternative. The thickly padded undercloth protected the table surface; no mats were necessary. Now mats have superseded cloths: centre-piece, individual place mats, mats for finger-bowls and glasses can be completely of tatting, or trimmed with it. Table napkins, if plain, can carry a border. For the tea-table there are tray cloths of all sizes; the tea-cosy still survives, and can carry a loose cover of tatting over silk or other material.

In more general furnishings, the one-time antimacassar, now the 'chair-back', is still in use. The Victorian window blind, with its border of coarse 'blind lace', has now been replaced by light net curtains: these can carry a small narrow edging. Parchment lamp-shades can be decorated with small motifs glued on to them, either outside, or on the inner surface: a silk shade can be covered with tatting (of a rather open pattern) or carry a border around the upper or lower edge. As the light is behind these motifs, colours will not show, and white thread will not be definite enough. Black is the most effective, especially if applied inside the shade.

The old-time blotting book was often covered with a plain linen loose cover, embroidered. In the absence of a blotting book, the loose cover has been transferred to the *Radio Times*. Tatting can here take the place of the embroidery.

Motifs in suitable threads and colours can be applied to church vestments and furnishings: a chalice veil, maniple, markers, etc. These formed a large part of the work of Queen Marie, in whose time the vestments of the Greek Orthodox Church were very richly decorated with lace and jewels.

There are indeed many possible forms of application, more perhaps than for any other type of needlework. Purely decorative pieces can be laid under glass (table-tops, trays, etc.) or mounted and framed as a picture, like many forms of embroidery; but unlike embroidery they can be removed, added to and rearranged in a new manner, or on a new background, as often as you wish.

MATERIALS AND TOOLS

Threads and their properties

Smoothness, suppleness and firmness are the essential properties of threads suitable for tatting. Their thickness is a matter of choice: theoretically any pattern can be worked in any thickness. Threads of cotton, linen, silk, artificial products and a foundation thread covered with metallic foil (an inexpensive substitute for real gold thread) fulfil these requirements in varying degrees.

Cotton (mercerized or not) is the most commonly used at the present time. There are several British makes, sold under the title of 'crochet cotton'. It is obtainable in a number of thicknesses and colours. A well-known French make of 'tatting cotton' is available in many soft colours but in a fine gauge only. For a very fine thread, sewing cotton (of which 'Sylko' is an example) can also be used, and there is a good range of colour. It tangles easily, and stretches more than crochet cotton: it is only suggested for very small decorative pieces.

In selecting cottons, beginners are advised to use No. 20, but No. 40 is a good average size, with 60, 70, 80 and upwards for finer work.

Linen threads are not so easy to work as cotton, as they are stiffer and not quite so smooth, but they give a pleasant 'bloom' to the work. They are available in very few gauges and colours, but they can be dyed. Certain linen threads used in lace-making are not suitable for tatting – the thread is fluffy and too irregular to draw up. Queen Marie and Lady Hoare both used linen threads, and it is recommended in modern German patterns.

Silk has been used from quite early times, as it was a feature of Riego's work, and

XI

XII

XIII

PLATE XI THE TUDOR ROSE (*page* 54)

PLATE XII ROCOCO ROSE (*page* 54)

PLATE XIII THE DAISY CHAIN (*page* 54)

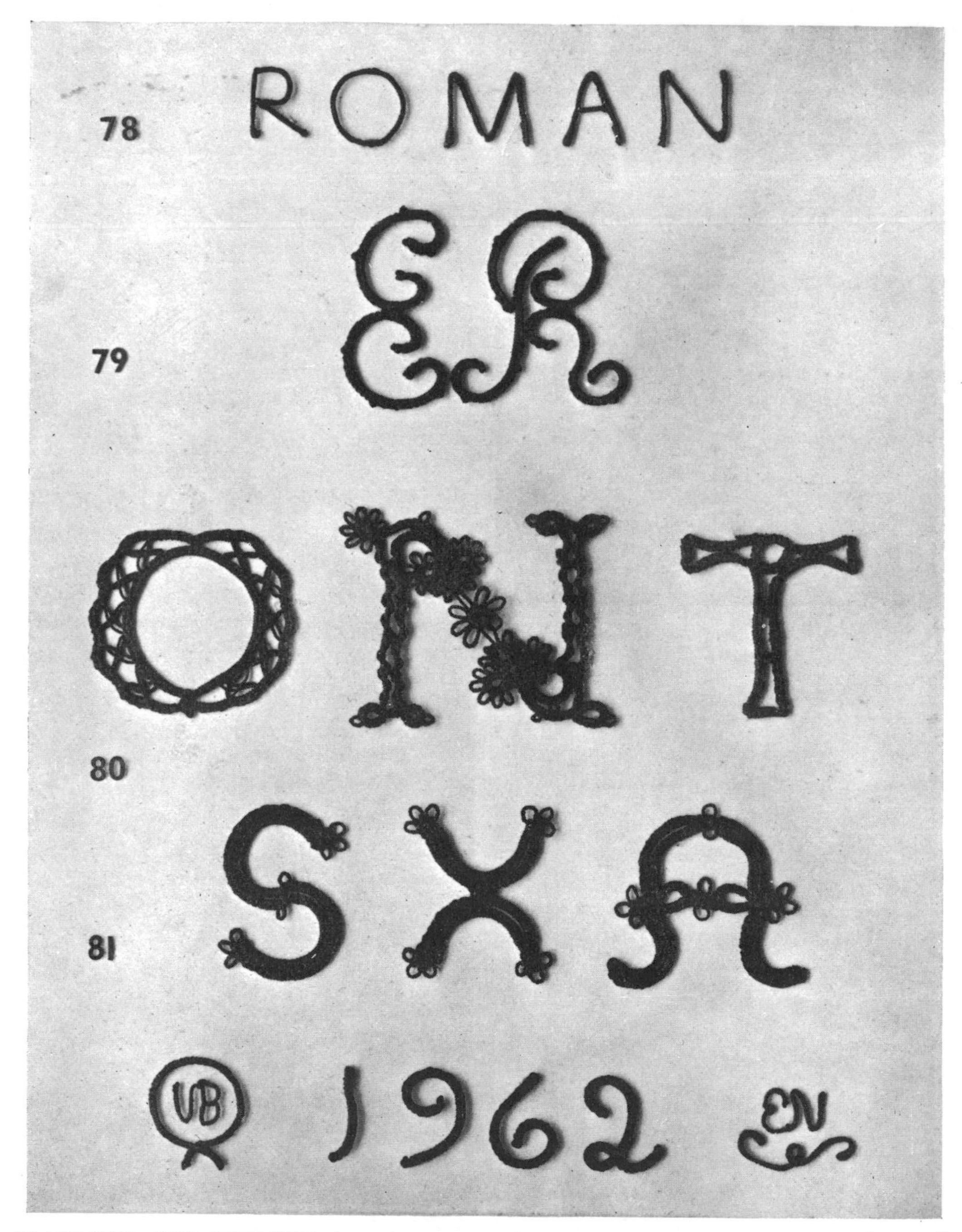

PLATE XIV THE ALPHABET AND ARITHMETICAL FIGURES · FIGURES 78–81 (*page* 56)

also of Queen Marie's richer pieces. There is no silk really suitable for the purpose today, but sewing silk can be used for small pieces (e.g. ornament for a silk handkerchief). In making up, it is slightly thicker than 'Sylko'. It makes graceful, supple picots: the thread is resilient and soft. Both 'Sylko' and real silk are best used for making small rings with large picots. A chain of silk is inclined to lose its lustre owing to the close packing of the stitches.

Terylene (gauge 200) being synthetic is the most uniform of all threads: it is very fine and suitable only for very precise workers. It lies very flat when at correct tension, but is difficult to work because it stretches and is inclined to twist.

Metallic threads: All threads for tatting must be round; most metallic threads for machine and hand embroidery are flat. There are, however, untarnishable 'gold' and 'silver' round threads which are quite satisfactory. Gold 'twist' was used by Riego on several occasions, and again by Queen Marie, for her ecclesiastical work.

Shuttles

There are various types of shuttles obtainable but none so good as the original hand-made specimens of bone, ivory, tortoise-shell or mother-of-pearl, all of which were beautifully balanced and take a fine polish. These are sometimes to be found in antique shops, their size indicating their date. It has already been pointed out that the size of the shuttle bears no relation to the size of the tatting stitch, this being dependent on the thickness of the thread. A small shuttle is more convenient when using a fine thread, and vice versa. Materials used today are imitation tortoise-shell, various forms of plastic, and steel.

The shuttle consists of a central block, usually pierced with a hole, in which the thread is knotted, and two flat blades enclosing the block, ending in closely aligned jaws at both ends. These must have a certain amount of 'spring' and remain closed, otherwise when the shuttle is 'spun' to recover an unravelled thread, the thread will unwind automatically from the open jaws. The weight and balance of the shuttle is important: some are so light that they tend to fly out of the hand when working at speed. Some are too slippery, some are too convex for convenience, while the steel, though a popular one, is rather heavy. This has a detachable spool which can be wound on a sewing machine: this saves a good deal of time but is awkward if it is required to make rings and chains alternately at frequent intervals, as the length of the thread between it and the work cannot be easily adjusted. The beginner should try several of different types, choosing the one which for her is the best balanced and most comfortable to hold, working at speed. As several shuttles will be needed, this is not an extravagance.

Lady Hoare describes some very fine, large shuttles which are in the Wallace collection, and some in Paris. 'One is of cut, pierced and wrought steel with a monogram of flowers that shows it belonged to Madame Louise, the daughter of Louis XV. One is of rock crystal mounted in gold and set with garnets; another, of earlier date, of gold in three tints framing beautiful little figure subjects in enamel; a third, also of gold, in three tints, pierced and chased with garlands of leaves tied with bows.' The Musée de Cluny has some very fine ones, 'one of six inches in length, of gold and red lacquer with a pair of lovers on it in Louis XVI costume'. The contemporary plastic models would appear to be less glamorous, but no less efficient in capable hands.

It might here be mentioned in passing that in the Pitt-Rivers Museum, Blandford, Dorset, there is a case with the general label of 'Remains of Goths, Visigoths and Franks from the Continent, A.D. 200–800'. A small collection in this case is labelled 'Objects of Roman manufacture found with remains of barbarian invaders at Mayence'. One of these objects is a bone shuttle, 4 inches in length, the greatest width 0·9 inches. It is not stated whether the shuttle is of Roman or Barbarian origin. If tatting had not then evolved as a craft, it is possible that the shuttle was used for making nets, by either party, for nets were part of primitive man's equipment for both attack and defence. If Roman, it could conceivably have been used for making a fabric formed of decorative knots: that they were tatting knots is open to conjecture. This substantiates the suggestion that tatting first arose in Italy, but the date is put back by several hundred years. It could of course, have been evolved, died out, and evolved again several times between then and the sixteenth century.

Other tools

A pair of sharp pointed scissors, a fine steel crochet hook, sewing needles, plated brass pins and a board for stretching the work, complete the list of tools.

The hands

The hands actually hold the thread and make the stitch, and their condition is important: they must at all times be clean and dry. Thread tightens when wet: if a drop of moisture falls on to the ring in process of making, the stitches will contract and it will not pull up. The work has to be handled both lightly and firmly: to draw up a ring the work is close between finger and thumb, and perspiration marks are liable at these points. Perspiration on white cotton always shows: it is resistant to boiling in soap solution or any other detergent, and chlorine bleaches only intensify the black shadow of the stain. When a soiled white edging is applied to a white linen handkerchief the contrast is only too apparent.

CHAPTER II

Making the Stitch

Winding the shuttle

TO thread or wind, pass the end of the thread through the hole in the centre block and knot it, cutting off the free end closely. Wind the thread evenly: for practice it need not be filled, but if it is, no thread should protrude past the edge of the blades or the thread would become rubbed when working; and an overloaded shuttle causes the blade tips to open. If by mistake the thread becomes caught over the face of one of the blades, unwind back to this point and rewind. Cut off the ball.

Holding the shuttle

The active or working shuttle is held in the right hand like a pencil, blade uppermost. It has no back or front, being the same at both ends, until it is held in the hand; then the tip held by the finger and thumb is referred to as the back. The thread should leave the shuttle from the side farthest away from you, at the back.

You will be passing the shuttle over and under a taut thread held in the left hand. The shuttle must be held firmly but lightly enough so that this thread, whether above or below the blade, slips smoothly between it and the fingers (above) or thumb (below). Hence the necessity for leaving the blade clear of loose ends or threads caught across them from careless winding.

Tension of threads

This comes with practice, and its importance will be better understood when you have made a few rings and chains. When making the stitch, you are always using two threads from the point of view of tension. Either can be too slack or too tight. A slack shuttle thread in a ring means it is not pulled up completely, while in a chain its natural curve has not been achieved, and it is too long. Unwanted picots will appear if the thread making the knots is too slack, and if too tight, a ring will be very difficult to draw up – the stitches strangle it and the thread may break. It is essential to have complete control over both threads to produce even work.

Making the stitch

Various tatting books may differ slightly in their methods of making the stitch. It does not matter which system you use, the only object being to choose the way which you can follow from the book, if you are teaching yourself, and can work easily and at speed. Most tatting books give instructions for making the ring first and the chain second. The stitch of course is the same in both, the shuttle thread forming the running line: in the ring, a distant part of the shuttle thread forms the stitches, while in the chain they are made of a second thread, either attached to the ball, or wound on to another shuttle. Where there are two threads, they may be of different colours (e.g. black and white) so that the transference of the knot may be more clearly seen, an advantage for beginners: instructions are therefore given for making a chain of two colours for the sake of practice. (The distinction does not show in the drawing.)

To make a chain with two coloured threads

Take a shuttle wound with black thread, and tie the free end to a length of white thread (about two yards for practice, or work direct from the ball) with a reef knot. Hold the reef knot between the first finger and thumb of the left hand, the black

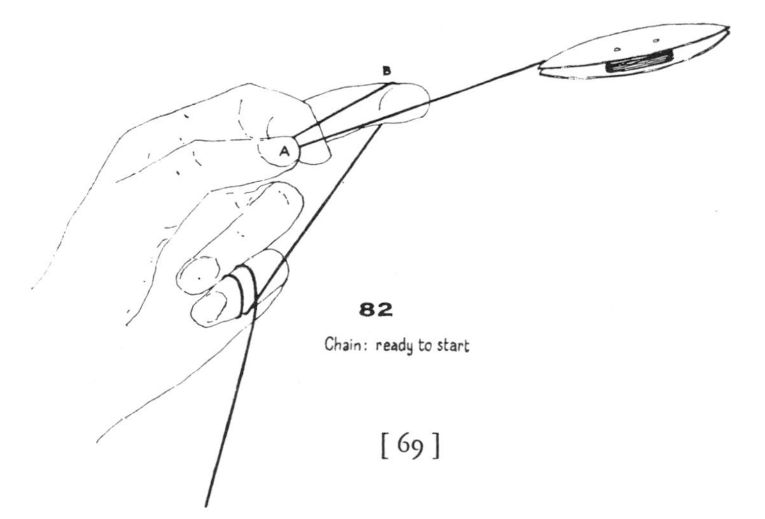

82

Chain: ready to start

thread nearest to you: pass the white thread behind the slightly extended middle finger of the same hand, then twist it twice round the little finger to steady it. You will now have a taut line about two inches in length between the reef knot (A) and the middle finger (B). This is the section on which the knot will first be made: by extending and relaxing the middle finger the thread can be tightened or slackened. The drawing shows the left hand in position.

Adjust the shuttle so that there is not more than nine inches of thread (preferably less) between it and the reef knot, holding it as described previously.

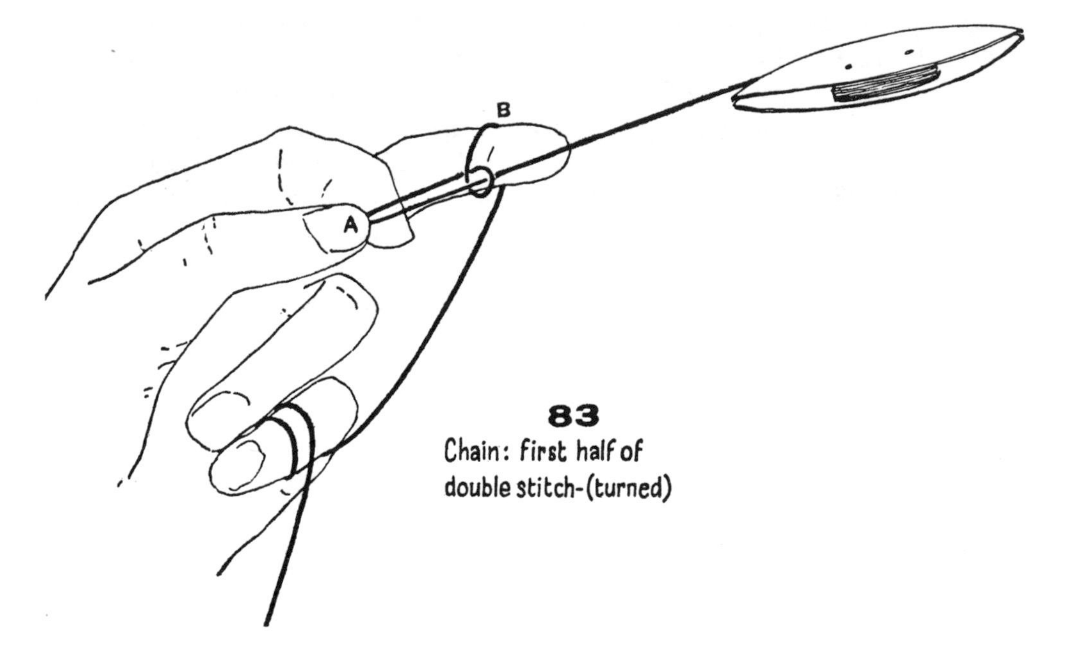

83
Chain: first half of double stitch-(turned)

The first half of the double stitch: Pass the shuttle thread behind the little finger of the right hand to steady it. Bring the shuttle up to the left hand and slip it *under* the taut line AB as if you were lifting it. When the back end of the shuttle is just clear, bring it back again (without turning it round) but *over* the taut white line and under the black thread (i.e. itself), slackening the taut line so that a (black) knot is formed upon it about an inch away from the reef knot under the thumb: if closer it will not have room to turn. With a slight sharp *lifting* movement tighten the shuttle thread, slipping it free from the little finger: the knot will be transferred on to the other thread, resulting in a white knot lying on the black thread.

Push the stitch hard up against the reef knot by tightening the white thread and pulling gently on the black, raising the shuttle slightly: most beginners try to hold the shuttle vertically before the knot is turned, which it cannot do if the shuttle is held up too high. Make several of these half-stitches, sliding them up closely together. If you make too many the chain will begin to develop a twist (you are really making Figure 51) as they are all facing one way. When the second half of the stitch is made the twist will be compensated and the chain will remain straight.

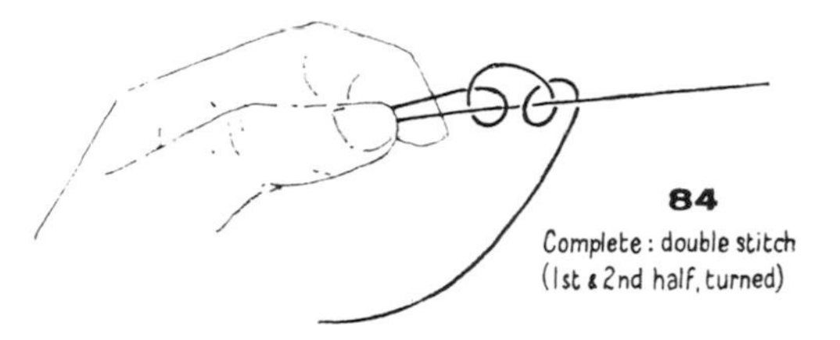

84
Complete: double stitch
(1st & 2nd half, turned)

The second half of the double stitch: Bring up the shuttle as before, but this time instead of passing *under* the taut line carry the shuttle *over* it and return under (the reverse of the first), pressing the black shuttle thread down out of the way with the thumb of the left hand. Transfer the knot as before. The first half of the stitch is a right-hand turn, the second is a left one: the drawing shows the second after turning, following a first, i.e. a complete double stitch. Both of course must be tight round the running thread, and pushed up into position under the thumb. After a few stitches, move the finger and thumb along the chain, to give you more control.

Making a ring

As the same thread has to do duty for both running line and taut thread, it is one colour only.

Lay the shuttle thread across the palm of the left hand, free end downwards, and hold it firmly between the first finger and thumb. The point at which you hold it is called the starting point, and is equivalent to the reef knot in the previous instructions for the chain. Carry the thread over the middle finger of the left hand, extending the finger so that there is about two inches of taut thread between it and the starting

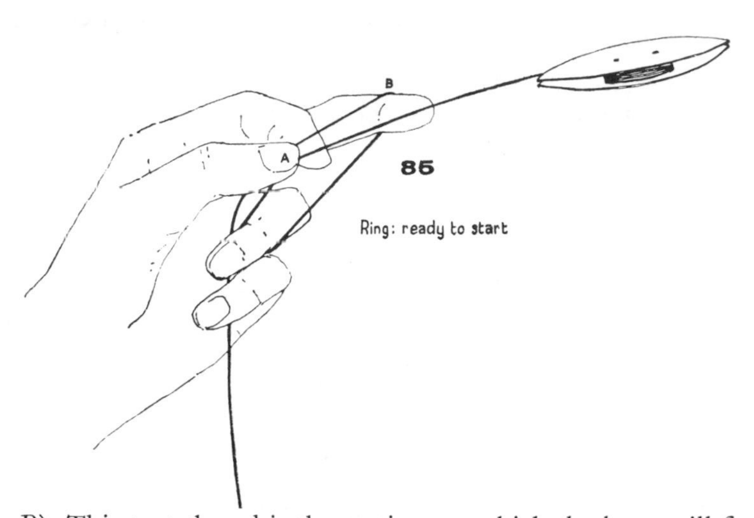

85

Ring: ready to start

point (A to B). This taut thread is the section on which the knot will first be made. By extending or relaxing the middle finger this section will be tightened or slackened as necessary. Take the thread on, behind the third finger and up to the starting point again, gripping it with the finger and thumb: you now have a triangle of thread, held in shape by three fingers: this triangle becomes the ring when a sufficient number of stitches have been worked on it. Before you attempt to make the stitch, stretch the second and third fingers, still gripping the two threads under the thumb, but allowing one of them to move freely so that the triangle is made bigger: make it smaller by pulling the shuttle thread. Do this several times until you are familiar with the feel of the triangle and can control its size. The drawing shows the triangle in position ready for the stitch.

To make the first half of the double stitch on the ring: Hold the shuttle as previously described, with about nine inches of thread between it and the starting point: steady the thread by passing it behind the little finger (of the right hand) and slip the shuttle *under* the taut thread of the triangle (A–B). When it is just clear, bring it back *over* the thread, and under the thread nearest to you, bending the middle finger so that the taut thread is slackened. It will be carrying the knot which you have just made. Pull the shuttle with a slight lifting movement: the shuttle thread now becomes the running line again and carries the knot which it originally made. Let the stitch slip back to the starting point under the thumb and hold it there. So far the starting point has been in name only: now it has a stitch to mark its position. It will stay in this position as soon as the second half-stitch is made.

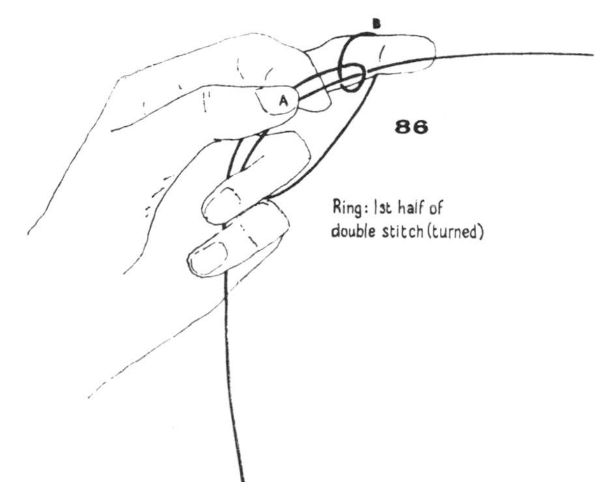

To make the second half of the double stitch on the ring: Bring the shuttle up to the taut thread as before but this time *over* it and return *under* it. Slacken the thread and transfer the knot as before: you now have a complete double stitch, as made in Figure 84.

Make at least ten doubles before attempting to pull them up into a ring. When you have made enough, release the left hand, pick up the work in the left hand between the finger and thumb so that when you pull you are not stretching the ring open (i.e. put the thumb on the beginning and end of the line of stitches), and pull firmly until all the excess thread of the triangle has disappeared and the ring is 'closed'. Once closed it cannot open again.

Practise making several rings, of different sizes: remember that if you have failed to transpose one of the stitches it will not pull up. Beginners should test every stitch by stretching the triangle between each: if the triangle will not enlarge then you have a locked stitch. The triangle will get smaller with every stitch made, as it is being used up to make them: keep it a convenient size by drawing more thread from the shuttle. Speed is achieved by working with a large triangle and a short shuttle thread: the tendency at first is to work with the shuttle thread too long.

The Josephine ring

Made as the ordinary ring, but all the stitches are of one (either) kind. Practise these of eight or ten single stitches, pulling them up very carefully to get a good circle, pressing them into position with the thumbnail. (A Josephine ring is shown in Figure 4 in the first part of the book.)

To make a picot

As described in Figure 7 a picot is formed by making a double stitch the required length away from the stitch before it, that is, by making the first half and turning it, but not sliding it up until the second half locks it into position. When drawn up, the picot will be half the length of the distance left between the stitches. Picots can be measured by holding the taut thread against a measured scale, the teeth of a comb, or more conveniently against a row of pins stuck in the edge of a board. After a little practice picots can be measured exactly, but begin by making a number of the same (short) length by eye, between every two or three doubles. A ring cannot start directly with a picot, neither can it end with one, since a double stitch on both sides is required to hold it.

You have now made a ring, a chain, and can form a picot on either. The next step is to join, through the picot, rings or chains to one another. Before doing so, it is necessary to recognize in which direction the stitches lie on the second piece, in relation to the first to which it is joined.

Direction of stitches

A line of stitches has two sides, one carrying more threads than the other: on this side the picots are made. This side could be called the 'face', and therefore the line 'faces' in one direction or another, i.e. up or down, in or out, in relation to another ring or chain. As you work, the line is facing outwards (or upwards), and the diagrams show this. In a ring, the stitches necessarily face outwards, but a chain may face up or down, according to the design. (If they are required to face down, the usual instruction is to 'reverse work', i.e. turn the work over so that the stitches will face in the opposite direction.)

At a join, the first ring made carries the picot: the second one (during its making) joins into it. A loop is made of *either* the triangle round the hand, *or* of the shuttle thread itself, pulled through the picot, and the shuttle thread passed through the loop to hold it there. Which of the two threads is used depends on whether the two lines of stitches are facing one another, or both facing in the same direction. In other words you form the loop from the thread which is nearest to the picot: thus you avoid crossing them, and so can keep the join flat.

To join into a picot where the stitches on both pieces face one another (as in ring to ring)

During the making of the second ring, when ready to join, sufficient thread from the triangle is pulled as a loop (from underneath) through the picot with a hook: the loop must be large enough to pass the shuttle through it. Then pull the shuttle thread gently until it is taut and held by the loop: stretch the triangle until the loop disappears from sight, and the second ring is close against the picot. This drawn-through loop counts as the first half of a double stitch. Follow with the second half. This 'pair' counts as a double belonging to the section between this picot and the next. (If the loop were not included, the resultant ring would be larger than a ring with no joins, since the loop occupies a place on the running thread.)

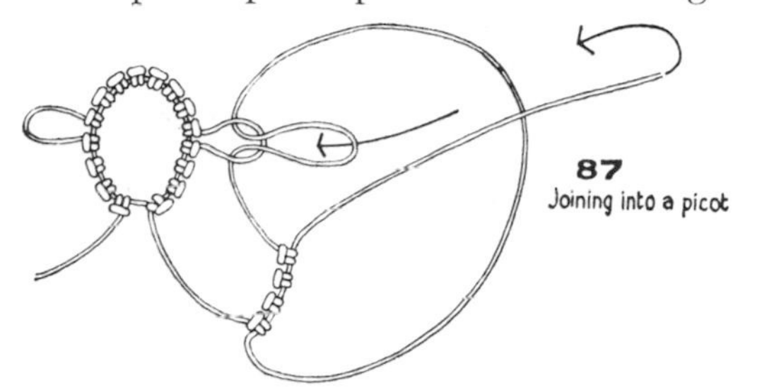

87
Joining into a picot

It is important that the join is a perfectly clean one: both threads must be taut – they need to be pulled alternately against one another until they settle into position, leaving no odd loops on either thread. It is of course essential that the loop does not get twisted, or a locking stitch results by mistake. Make sure that the running thread is running freely after the join. Joining into a picot on a ring, by another ring, is shown in Figure 87.

For practice, make a row of rings, carrying spaced picots, and join them, as in Figure 34. Work five doubles or more between each picot.

To join the last ring to the first in a circle

Figure 34 can be pulled round into a circle, so that the last ring joins on to the picot first made on the first ring. It is joined in exactly the same manner, but it is a little more difficult to hold the work. Make sure that the loop is drawn through from the back, as before, and make sure that the triangle and shuttle threads are on the front of the work. Practise making rows of rings, joined together, and practise joining this last picot, as you will meet with this frequently.

To join two lines of stitches, both facing in the same direction

Since chains can face in either direction, those that face one another will be joined in the same manner as ring to ring, described above: but where they face the same way, in parallel lines or circles, the running thread of the second-made chain will be nearest to the picot carried on the first one, and this must form the loop. On arrival at the picot, pull up the chain to the required tension (you cannot tighten it afterwards); draw the active shuttle thread through the picot, and, holding the work tightly so that the thread does not slip, pass the shuttle thread through the loop of itself, which must not be twisted, as it tends to become. Pull the shuttle thread tightly so that the knot settles firmly into the picot. The second thread has taken no part in the operation but is ready in position for making the next section of the chain. (Figure 53 is joined in this manner.)

This method must be used when a chain is joined to a ring and the chain is facing away from it, as under such a condition the running thread is again nearest to the picot on the ring.

Not all the examples in the illustrations are correctly worked. In Figure 60, the Italian edging, the chain around the centrally placed scallop shows a distinct 'lift' at the joins, which is wrong. In the following figure, No. 61, composed of concentric chains all facing outwards, the joins are correct and lie flat. This method of joining is always described in German patterns, which use a great many chains in their construction.

Beginner's practice

Before attempting this join, which is more difficult than joining ring to ring, go back to the ring alone, and make clovers (Fig. 41) which are excellent lessons in rings of different sizes, and spaced joined picots. Then make rings for the centre of medallions, bearing a given number of equal length picots. If the ring requires picots between every two doubles, start the ring with one double: make the picots with two doubles between each, and finish with one double: when drawn up there will be two doubles between each picot. When you have made such a ring, carrying eight picots, work the daisy (Fig. 42) joining the rings to one another. This will also be practice for joining with the running thread, in preparation for joining chain to chain, to be attempted later.

CHAPTER III

The Continuous Thread

OLDER pattern books, and many foreign ones, describe the use of the continuous thread, which has several advantages. As a general rule, instructions for making a chain require the ball and shuttle threads to be tied together at the start of the work, or at the point where the first chain is to be made. It is more logical not to cut off the ball after the shuttle is wound, but to continue working with the thread still attached to the ball or, better in most circumstances, wound on to a second shuttle. You are therefore beginning work in the middle of a length of thread instead of at one end, i.e. two shuttles are wound, starting at the opposite ends of the thread, until they meet. If the design starts with a ring, it is made by either shuttle: if a chain follows it, the second thread is ready to hand. This second shuttle can either supply the second thread or can be transferred to the right hand and become the active one, according to the effect you want. (See the scrolls, Figs. 62, 63 and 64.) By this method the initial join is eliminated and there is greater control of the tension over the whole piece of work.

Where a design starts with a chain, make the smallest possible knot in the space of thread between the two shuttles: do this by making a loop and passing one shuttle through it: pull it up tightly. You have now made a 'holding knot', which you place under the thumb of the left hand, and proceed as in the chain already described (made of two coloured threads): the knot will be the starting point. Make sure that no inadvertent picots appear (which they tend to do at the beginning) by pushing together the first few stitches very tightly. You can only do this by dropping the whole piece of work and pressing the knots together with the fingers. All the models shown which begin with the chain have been worked in this manner. A picot can be made immediately if needed: the small holding knot keeps it in place. This formation is much used in free-style work, and is described as 'to start with a picot at the head of a chain'. Riego, as we have seen, used the continuous thread and often started with a very small ring (oeillet) to neaten the end, before beginning the chain.

A well-made chain is neat and tight, and is started as closely as possible to the ring before it. This is no problem if ring and chain are being worked on alternate shuttles. It is more difficult if one shuttle is making them both.

Further applications of the continuous thread

Rings in series: This is a further application but rather beyond the scope of the beginner. It is not easy to make a row of rings very closely to one another, as in the basic shapes. (The diagrams show them some distance apart but in practice they would be as close as possible.) If a second shuttle is used this can make a half-stitch over the first shuttle thread between the rings: the rings are then carried on a 'chain' of single stitches, whose running thread is continuous throughout the circle: it can therefore be pulled up very tightly, and more compactly, in spite of the additional half-stitches between the rings. If a clover is made between two chains, a half-stitch between the clover rings keeps them neatly together.

'Climbing out' of a ring through a picot

This is an old method, used by Riego, and recently revived. In a pattern where a following round (on two threads) is connected to picots on a ring previously worked (as in a medallion, central ring type), this following round can be worked on the same pair of threads as the central ring. (Not the same as the daisy, where the whole is on only one thread.)

Make the central ring on a continuous thread, but with one picot less than the number required. On drawing up, the threads will be lying together as usual. With these threads make a knot at a short distance from the ring, i.e. a distance equalling the length of a picot. There will thus be formed the final picot and the threads are now in position for beginning the following round with a chain, or a ring, provided the ring faces outwards. This method dispenses with the cutting of the thread after the central ring, and also makes it possible to produce one with picots between every double stitch, with all picots evenly spaced.

UNPICKING, JOINING THREADS, ENDING OFF

A ring may be unpicked if it has not been drawn up, but not afterwards. A blunt needle or pin is inserted between the stitches one at a time, the path of the shuttle carefully reversed. This is very tedious, the thread soon becomes unravelled, and it takes a long time. It is not worth unpicking more than a few stitches: it is better to cut clear, cutting through the offending ring near its end, when there will be just enough thread on pulling out on which to tie a new one. If the ring has been attached to a picot, the thread can be disengaged – never cut through a picot.

A chain may be undone rather more easily, or cut so that it will leave enough thread on which to join the new one – its running thread will be very short. You cannot of course make a join in the middle of a chain; it must be cut back to the nearest ring: if there is no ring in the design you must either cut out the whole section of chain or make the join where it engages with a picot, which is not so satisfactory.

Joining threads

Joining during working may be necessary for several reasons: the shuttle may have run out, there may be a flaw in the cotton, a thread of another colour is required, or a mistake has been made which cannot be undone. At the join, which should be made at the base of a ring or the beginning of a chain, there will be two ends which must not show. One may be worked over for a few stitches as the work proceeds, tucking it in to lie parallel with the running thread, and then cut off short: the other may be either worked over (if the design permits) or threaded into a needle and darned through the nearest stitches at the back.

Ending off

As there is no opportunity for working in the final end(s), the work being completed, they must be darned into the back and cut off. If the piece is very tightly worked, the thread may be separated into strands and so a finer needle used. A neat finish is as important in tatting as in any other needlework. It is not easy but is worth the care and attention that should be given to it.

Individual methods of work

A few workers become masters of some particular aspect of tatting, which they make their speciality. They develop an individual way of making the stitch, drawing up rings and other operations, which depends on certain movements, angle of thread, etc., for which no written description or drawing would be adequate. Attention to these finer points make the really expert tatter, but such methods can only be learnt successfully from their originators.

CHAPTER IV

Patterns

Systems of pattern description

ONCE you have started work, you are following a pattern, and there is more than one way of writing it: it is important to know the system you are following. A pattern is an instruction for working and should be as concise and clear as the language can make it, allowing no possibility for mistake. Patterns for beginners must of course include every detail, but for more advanced workers something more brief should suffice. It is an advantage if the actual pattern is preceded by a brief description of the design as a whole. This gives a grasp of what the designer is intending to convey and can shorten the subsequent directions. Most English patterns do not give this, but the directions are very complete and leave nothing to chance: they can be followed stitch by stitch although they make rather laborious reading, i.e. the result is difficult to visualize. Many foreign patterns on the other hand give a good general outline but omit the details concerning joining which the worker has to assume from the illustration. French patterns are extremely brief, owing partly to the conciseness of the language. To indicate a chain, they merely state: 'with two shuttles', from which it is inferred that a chain will result. 'With one shuttle' indicates a ring. Frequently they announce: 'for the order in which the rings are to be worked, consult the diagram', which is disconcerting to the beginner.

German patterns give the rings and chains by numbers in order of working. This is useful in long patterns, when it is easy to lose one's place. Australians transpose the half-stitches and make the second one first. (This makes no real difference as either way the stitches make a pair.)

The real difficulty in all languages is giving instructions for making a picot. The picot is not a stitch, it is a space, but it requires a stitch to define the space, i.e. to form it. The question arises, is the stitch which makes it to be included in the number of stitches which follow, or is it not. Unfortunately there is no international ruling on this. (This problem of accurate description would not have arisen if we had kept to Riego's original method of making the picot between the two halves of a double stitch, which was called 'the picot stitch' and was independent of the number on either side of it.)

The English method of description would appear to be the most satisfactory, that is, the stitch forming the picot is disregarded as such, and included in the number to be worked in the next section: therefore you work one less than is indicated. If it were counted, i.e. its presence observed, the number given would be one less, since one stitch is already worked. This latter system occurs in many foreign patterns and their translations and it is essential to know which you are following.

The ensuing patterns are written in a style slightly different from the usual method. Normally the direction for a ring or chain (whose picots are equally spaced) is written in the following manner: 'Make a ring of 5 doubles: 3 picots separated by 5 doubles: ending with 5 doubles.' It should be equally intelligible if the instructions read: 'Make a ring of 3 picots, each 5 doubles apart, total 20 doubles.' Since you cannot start or end with a picot, the opening and closing sections of 5 doubles have been assumed and taken as fact, thus shortening the description, which also gives a clearer picture of the size of the ring, and its picot spacing. Where the picot spacing is unequal, the description of course cannot be so concise.

In the patterns, an overall description of the design is given, followed by the length and construction of the repetitions composing it. They also endeavour to make clear the point at which you are starting the work.

EDGINGS AND BORDERS

The simplest pieces to make are edgings, which can be used as trimmings on clothing and handkerchiefs, and many household linens. Edgings may be very narrow or several inches in depth, in which case they qualify for the title of border. They may be composed of one or any number of rounds. (A one-round edging is not necessarily the simplest to work.) The gauge of the thread should be in proportion to the material which it trims, from fine handkerchiefs to coarse linen tablecloths. Thread No. 20 is suitable for 'heavy' work, and for beginners' practice: use from No. 60 onwards for more delicate pieces.

Every pattern book contains a page or more of edgings, which are in great variety, but not all show their corners, in that they are not always necessary (e.g. for round or oval mats, etc.): but the problem of making them will arise in edgings for handkerchiefs (usually the first pieces attempted) and many household linens. The construction of a right-angle has to be mastered; the pattern must not be unduly distorted and the work must lie flat. Very simple narrow edgings can be eased round a corner when sewing them on, so that no further adjustments need be made, but usually a corner motif has to be especially designed, appropriate to the style of the work. On a handkerchief carrying a very narrow edging, frequently one corner of the material is cut away and a large new motif introduced, which replaces it: this then becomes the dominant part of the trimming. The other three corners, if they cannot be eased, will need a special corner motif.

Two edgings are given here, with their corners: you should be able to work from the instructions and the diagrams (which are exaggerated to show the position of the joins into the picots). They are provided for practice in following directions and for turning the corners, both of which are very simple. The diagrams are very stylized and give no indication of the delicacy of the work. Read the preliminary descriptions carefully and check them with the diagram before beginning: observe the length of the repetition of the pattern, and how many rings and chains compose it. The rings are numbered in order of working for each repetition, and show their numbers in the diagram. The scroll, which in a modified form is the basis of a large number of edgings, is the principal theme in both.

A ONE-ROUND EDGING

Description: A scroll, with both rings and chains in two sizes. The rings are attached to the material which it trims.

Pattern repetition: Four small rings and one large one are connected to right and left with their neighbours. Two long chains, carrying two ornamental picots, lie on either side of the large ring. Three short chains, each with a central picot, lie between the long chains (total 5 rings, 5 chains).

Construction:

Small ring:	12 doubles in all, with 3 picots equally spaced, i.e. 3 doubles apart.
Large ring:	26 doubles in all: 9 doubles, join to picot of last ring, 4 doubles, picot, 4 doubles, picot, 9 doubles.
Short chain:	6 doubles, with one central picot.
Long chain:	9 doubles in all, with 2 picots equally spaced (3 doubles, picot, 3 doubles, picot, 3 doubles).

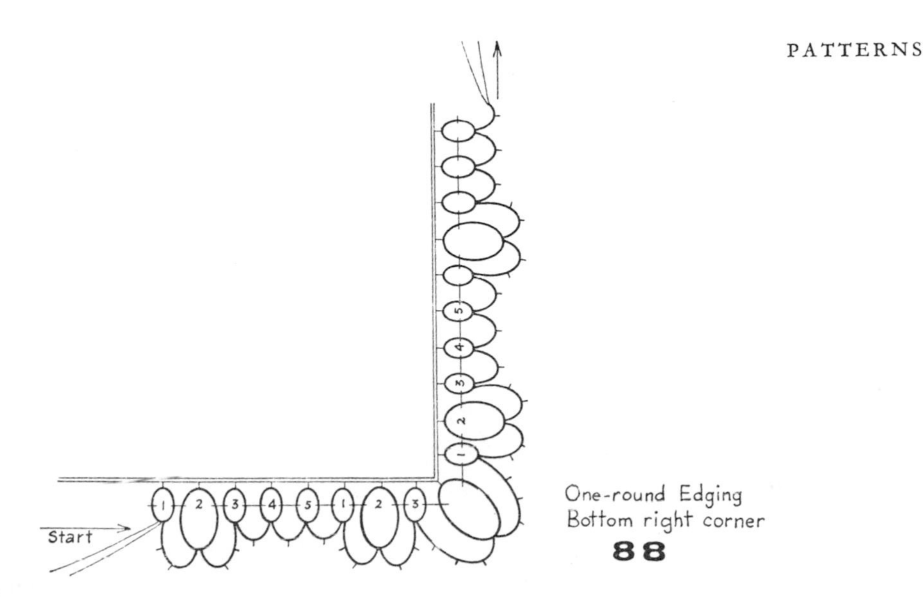

To work one repetition: Start with the small ring preceding the large one.

1st ring:	small ring as above (in ensuing repetitions join to the ring last made).
1st chain:	long chain as above.
2nd ring:	large ring as above.
2nd chain:	as first.
3rd ring:	as first, but joining to ring last made.
3rd chain:	short chain as above.
4th ring:	as third.
4th chain:	as third.
5th ring:	as third.
5th chain:	as third. This concludes a repetition.

The corner motif: A slightly larger ring, with a chain on either side carrying three ornamental picots, rests on the corner tip.

Corner ring: 12 doubles, join to picot of last ring, 3 doubles, picot, 3 doubles, picot, 12 doubles (total 30 doubles).

Corner chains: 3 picots, separated by 3 doubles (total 12 doubles).

A corner is made after the third ring of a repetition is completed. Instead of the third chain, make a corner chain: then the corner ring: then a second corner chain: this completes the corner. Begin the new side with the first ring of the repetition, and continue. The corner is then equally balanced on both sides. The diagram shows a bottom right-hand corner: working anti-clockwise along the lower edge, one repetition is shown; part of a second, up to and including the third ring; the corner motif; and up the right side, two complete repetitions.

A TWO-ROUND EDGING

The one shown is offered as practice in applying a second round whose length of repetition differs from that of the first.

Description of first round: A scroll of identical rings and chains. The rings are connected to one another and carry a central picot to which the second round is attached. The chains are attached to the fabric (instead of the rings as in the previous figure, therefore you will be working in a clockwise direction).

Pattern repetition: 1 ring, 1 chain.

Construction:

The ring: 3 picots separated by 5 doubles (total 20 doubles).

The chain: 1 central picot with 5 doubles on either side (total 10 doubles).

To work one repetition: Work a ring, as above, followed by the chain. This concludes a

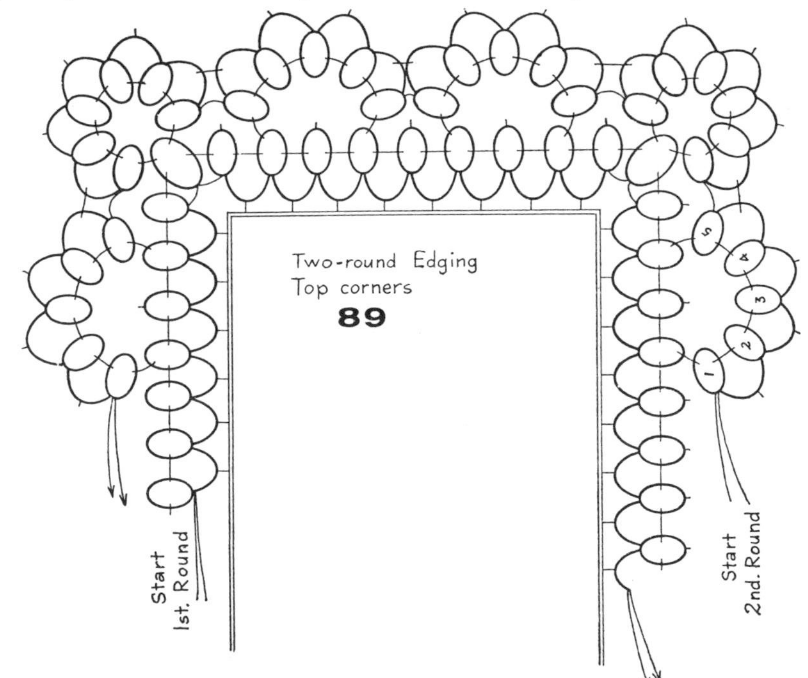

repetition. In ensuing repetitions, join the ring at its first picot position to the last picot of the preceding ring.

The corner: A ring directly on the corner is slightly larger than the others, carrying an extra picot: the corner proper consists of this one ring only, and thus interrupts the sequence of the scroll. It is joined on both sides to its neighbours. The result gives the appearance of a clover, but since the rings on either side are the same as those in the edging, these must belong to the description of the edging. After a ring of the edging, work the corner ring: 4 picots separated by 5 doubles (i.e. 5 doubles apart), total 25 doubles. Now begin a new repetition (with a ring). Continue round all four sides until the final chain meets the first ring made, joining the last ring into it. Since the second round has longer repetitions, each requiring the space of four rings on the first, the number of rings in the first round must be a multiple of four, plus one more on each of the four sides to balance the corner.

The diagram (Fig. 89) shows the scroll, started up the left-hand side, and its continuation round part of the fabric.

Description of second round: A series of scrolls, of identical rings and chains, are attached to alternate rings on the first round, forming slight scallops. It is not one long scroll, since after every fifth ring a chain is omitted, thus breaking the sequence of alternate ring and chain. As the scrolls are inverted (in relation to the first round) you will be working in an anti-clockwise direction (the reverse of the first round).

Pattern repetition: 5 rings, 4 chains.

Construction:

The ring: 7 doubles, picot, 5 doubles, picot, 7 doubles (total 19 doubles).

The chain: 1 central picot with 8 doubles on either side (total 16 doubles).

To work one repetition (i.e. one scroll): Start on the right-hand side with a ring (as above), joining at its first picot position into the fourth ring from the corner on the first round. Work a chain, as above, and continue with alternate rings and chains, joining the rings as you proceed, for four more rings: this last and fifth ring joins also into a ring on the first round, leaving one free ring between it and the one from which the repetition started. This concludes the repetition.

The corner scallop has one extra ring and chain. On arrival at the corner, start the repetition as usual, but join the first ring into the nearest picot on the corner ring. The first chain joins into the picot on the last chain of the previous repetition. Continue with ring and chain alternately, joining the sixth (and last) ring into the remaining picot on the corner ring: this concludes the corner.

Now start a third repetition, working along the upper edge, joining the first ring into the second small ring from the corner on the first round (there will thus be an unattached ring on either side of the corner), and joining the first chain into the last chain of the corner scallop. At the conclusion of the third, start the fourth, and continue with full repetitions until the next corner is reached.

The diagram shows, in addition to the first round, one (shortened) side and two corners.

This pattern, although appearing clumsy in the diagram, is very delicate in fine thread. A third round of one long chain with ornamental picots, and linking into the chain picots of the second, could be carried round the whole, to make it more elaborate. There is no limit to the rounds you may apply, provided they are made with regard to the lengths of the repetitions.

The two edgings described above are reasonably plain: they are planned for a lesson in following instructions, interpreting the diagrams, and for realizing the problems involved in the design and construction of right-angles. After edgings, the natural progression is the medallion, i.e. an edging pulled round into a circle: the following pattern consists of a mat in which again the scroll is the principal motif.

THE DAISY MAT

The early pieces of fabric were made of square, rectangular or circular shapes, worked independently and afterwards joined together. The daisy mat is an example of this formation, but the pieces are joined to one another as the work proceeds. The mat as worked consists of nine medallions: they are square with the exception of the centre one which is circular; this is optional. The whole is bordered by large clovers alternating with rounded scallops. The design is taken from the late Norma Benporath's Australian book, *Tatting Illustrated*, which contains a fine collection of mats of all kinds.

In both medallions the theme is the same: a central daisy, surrounded by a modified scroll. It is not an exact scroll, as at intervals the rings lie side by side with no intervening chain. There are two sizes of rings in both, and in the squares two sizes of chains.

The circular medallion

Description: A border of eight large rings, alternating with a pair of smaller ones, connected by a chain, surrounds the central daisy, to which the large rings are joined.

Construction: the daisy (see Fig. 42):

Central ring: 8 picots separated by 2 doubles (total 16 doubles).

On the same thread: ring of 28 doubles, with 3 picots equally spaced (7 doubles apart). Make a total of 8 rings, knotting the thread into a picot on the central ring between each. Join each ring after the first 7 doubles to the last picot of the ring preceding it; join the last ring to the first. Tie and cut on completion.

Construction: the border (eight repetitions):

Small ring: 3 picots separated by 3 doubles (total 12 doubles).
Large ring: 3 picots separated by 6 doubles (total 24 doubles).
The chain: 5 picots separated by 3 doubles (total 18 doubles).

To make one repetition (3 rings, 2 chains): Start with a large ring, as above, joining at centre into a daisy ring. In the following repetitions, join the large ring into the centre picot of the small ring preceding it.

The chain: as above.
Small ring: as above, joining at centre into last picot of large ring.
Small ring: as above, all picots free.
The chain: as above. This completes the repetition.

Make eight repetitions in all, bringing the last chain up to the base of the first ring, having joined the last small ring to the large ring first made. Tie and cut. This completes the circular medallion.

The square medallion

Description: The central daisy carries two types of rings: four are free and carry ornamental picots; the others are attached to the four large rings of the border. Between these border rings are two pairs of small rings, and chains of two sizes.

Construction: the daisy:

Central ring: 8 picots separated by 2 doubles (total 16 doubles).
1st ring: total of 28 doubles, with 3 picots 7 doubles apart.
2nd ring: total of 29 doubles: 7 doubles, join to picot of last ring, 5 picots 3 doubles apart, ending with 7 doubles. This gives the four ornamental picots and one for joining to the next ring.

Repeat these two rings alternately, joining them to one another, and joining the eighth and last ring to the first. Tie and cut.

Construction: the border (four repetitions):

Small ring: 5 picots separated by 3 doubles (total 18 doubles).

Large ring: 3 picots separated by 6 doubles (total 24 doubles).
Short chain: 5 picots separated by 3 doubles (total 18 doubles).
Long chain: 11 picots separated by 3 doubles (total 36 doubles).

To work one repetition (5 rings, 3 chains): Start in the centre of a side, with a large ring, as above, joining at centre into the first ring of the daisy.

Short chain: as above.
Small ring: as above, but joining at centre into last picot of last ring.
Small ring: as above: all picots free.
Long chain: as above: this forms the corner.
Small ring: as above, joining at centre into centre (third) picot of last ring.
Small ring: as above, all picots free.
Short chain: as above. This completes the repetition.

In the following repetitions join the large ring after the first 6 doubles into the centre picot of the ring preceding it. Work four repetitions in all, joining the last small ring to the first picot on the first-made large ring, and bringing the last chain up to its base. Tie and cut.

In the example (Plate XV) small rings of 8 or 9 picots immediately following one another have been sewn on to the centres of the daisies, to give a neater finish.

Assembly of medallions

These can be made and joined in any order, but it is easier if the circular one is worked first, the squares being joined into position during working. If the central one is circular, there will be an open space (roughly triangular) where three squares meet the circle.

Joining a square to a circle

The centre picots of the two short chains on the side of the square are joined to the centre picots of the chains on each side of the large ring in the border of the circle. (Strictly speaking this statement is inaccurate. The first-made chain (or ring) carries the picot: the chain that joins into it does not, i.e. two separate picots are not involved. Actually the chain joins at *the position* where its centre picot would be, if it carried one. As this would involve such a clumsy description the term 'centre picot' is usually employed, although it does not actually exist.)

Joining square to square

The centre picots of the two short chains on the side of a square are joined to a similar pair in a neighbouring square. This will cause the formation of a little diamond space with two free picots on each of its four sides. The long corner chains are joined to their opposites, by the third picot from the end (or the beginning) of the long chain. This will again produce a similar diamond, so that there will be three adjacent diamonds between the sides of the squares. When all the medallions are completed, work the outer border.

The Outer Border

There are two independent motifs: a scallop and the clover, alternately placed. They can be worked into position as they occur in the border, or all of one motif can be made first (preferably the scallop), filling in afterwards with the other.

The scallop: A large foundation ring is joined to the two short chains in the square border: attached to picots on this ring is a scroll. The first and last rings of the scroll (which are slightly smaller than the other four) are also attached to the short chains of the square. Its five chains are identical, the first and last joining to the clovers on either side.

The foundation ring:

2 doubles, join to fourth picot of short chain to the left of the large ring of the square border: 6 doubles: join to second picot of the next short chain (this gives a small triangular space with 1 free picot from each of the 2 chains): 4 doubles, picot, 4 doubles, picot, 10 doubles, picot, 4 doubles, picot, 10 doubles, picot, 4 doubles, picot, 2 doubles (total 46 doubles). Pull the ring up firmly, tie and cut.

The scroll: 6 rings, 5 chains.

Working anti-clockwise round the foundation ring, make the first ring:

4 doubles, join to second picot of the border chain: 4 doubles: join to the last-made picot on the foundation ring (this will give a very small triangle with 1 free picot): 3 doubles, picot, 3 doubles, picot, 3 doubles (total 17 doubles).

Work the chain, of 5 picots separated by 3 doubles (total 18 doubles).

Work the second ring:

5 picots separated by 3 doubles (total 18 doubles), joining at second picot to the last-but-one picot of the ring last made, and at centre to the next picot on the foundation ring.

The first and second rings of the scroll are thus joined together.

Work a second chain.

Work the third ring, like the second, except that it is not joined to the ring last made.

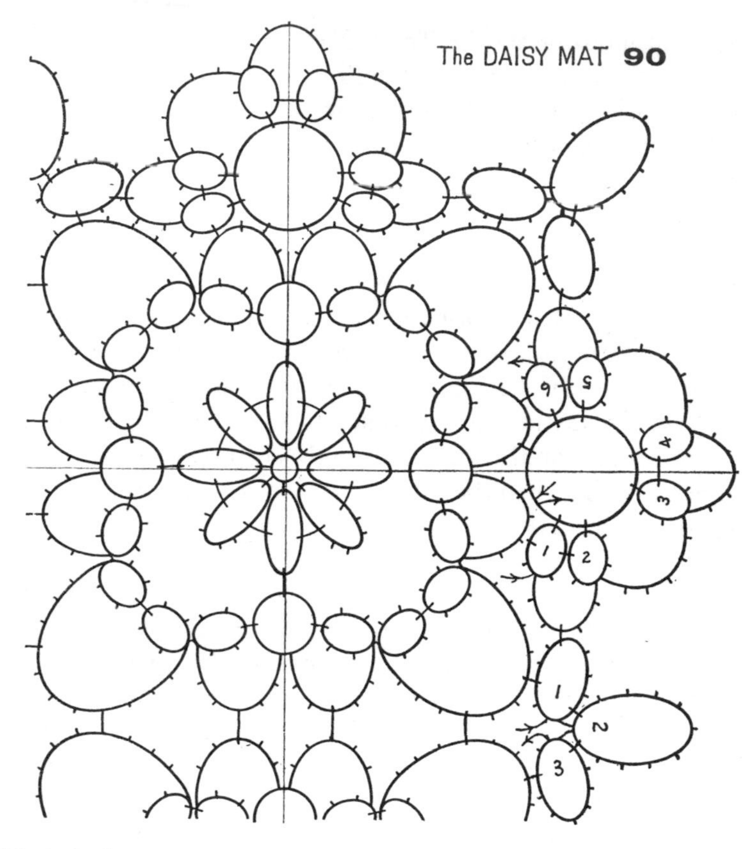

Work the third chain.

Work the fourth ring, as the second, following it with the fourth chain.

Work the fifth ring, as third, following it with the fifth (and last) chain.

Work the sixth (and last) ring the reverse of the first, joining to the ring last made: at its third picot to the foundation ring, and at its fourth and last picot to the fourth picot of the border chain, to the right of the large ring. Tie and cut.

This completes the scroll and the motif.

The clover:

1st ring	9 picots 3 doubles apart (total 30 doubles).
2nd ring:	3 doubles, join to last picot of last ring: continue for 10 picots, 3 doubles apart (total 36 doubles).

3rd ring: 3 doubles, join to last picot of last ring: continue for 8 picots, 3 doubles apart (total 30 doubles).

Tie and cut.

The first ring of the clover is joined at its second picot to the seventh picot of a corner chain of the square medallion: and at half-way to the centre picot of the first chain of the scallop scroll. Conversely, the last clover ring joins at half-way to the centre of the last chain of the next scallop, and at its eighth picot to the fifth picot of the corner chain of the next square. *The corner clover* is joined twice to the same corner chain, the second picot of its first ring joining to the seventh of this chain, the eighth picot of its last ring joining to the fifth of the same.

Figure 90 shows a corner of the Daisy Mat diagrammatically. It consists of one of the square medallions; two complete scallops; and two clovers, one of them the corner clover. The distances between formations have been exaggerated to show the joins more clearly. A photograph of the completed mat is given in Plate XV, but the piece is not well worked, and should not be consulted for the border joins, some of which are inaccurate.

A border makes a considerable difference to a mat, especially if the motifs composing it are rather plain. A border is really a glorified edging: in this particular case it consists of two independent motifs (one of them of two rounds) and is rather elaborate. A popular border is a row of half-wheels, which make a fine scallop (Fig. 43). They can be used alone, or they can alternate with clovers. Simpler to work are borders of one round, but these can appear just as elaborate: with rings and chains deep vandykes can be made, alternating with an arrangement of the scroll (e.g. Fig. 91), the whole on one pair of threads without a break. Simpler still is the effective and much used all-ring edging of rings on both sides of the thread: this gives a neat, cohesive appearance to the whole, forming a solid looking band. Figure 33, which demonstrated close joining by picot, was composed of three such rows in order to show just this effect. Here the spaces of thread between the rings are as short as possible: if the 'band' is required to border a circular piece, they and the picots must be longer.

CHAPTER V

Special Arrangements of Stitches

THE following descriptions are of some examples of arrangements of stitches and motifs, some now obsolete, some well known, and some new. With one or two exceptions only an example of the principle is shown, which the reader may recognize in patterns containing them, or incorporate in her own. Those described are: an application of the reversing chain, the long space of thread, crossing one line with another, the node stitch, multiple dead ends, pearl and raised tatting.

AN APPLICATION OF THE REVERSING CHAIN (Fig 91, Plate XVI)

An example of a reversing chain is shown in a scallop (developed from figure 50), which could be used as a border to a mat, repeated as it stands, or alternating with another motif. Unlike the scallop in the daisy mat (Fig. 90), it has the advantage of being composed on one pair of threads, which are in position for the next which follows it.

It is composed of the scroll, of four identical rings and three chains, two of which are long and form 'S' bends. The lower bend carries eight ornamental picots (one or two would be attached to the foundation mat) and the upper bend has five. It is also attached to the rings preceding and following it, by joining into the first, and making a picot for the second (not yet made). In the example, and for demonstration only, the motif has been worked on a continuous thread of black and white, with the reversing chain in black to show it more clearly. Also to show it more clearly, the joining picots which it carries, and the picots on the rings to which it joins, have been made longer. (To compensate for this the picot joining the second and third rings is also longer.) There are therefore both black and white picots, which enable you to see their place of origin.

Construction:

The ring: 5 picots separated by 3 doubles (total 18 doubles).

Reversing chain: (black) 3 doubles, picot, continue for 9 picots, making the last one longer. Now reverse direction of stitches for the bend. Join to centre picot of last ring; continue for 5 picots (all separated by 3 doubles, total 48 doubles).

Short chain: (white) 5 picots separated by 3 doubles (total 18 doubles).

To work one repetition: (4 rings, 3 chains):

Start with a ring: as above, lower left of scallop.

Reversing chain: as above.

2nd ring: as above, but joining at centre to the long picot on the reversing chain: the next (fourth) picot is a long one.

Short chain: as above.

3rd ring: as above, joining at second picot to long picot on the previous ring: the next (centre) picot is a long one.

Reversing chain: as above, but starting with 6 picots (instead of 9) and ending with 8 (instead of 5).

4th ring: as above, joining at centre into long picot of previous chain.

This motif is a good one for circular and oval borders, as the lower bends of the chains can be eased together or stretched farther apart when rounding a curve. The reversing chain can appear with advantage in narrow edgings, lying parallel to the edge of the fabric.

THE LONG SPACE OF THREAD (Mignonette) (Figs. 92–93, Plate XVI)

If, when working with one shuttle only, an extra long space of thread is left between each ring, forming a loop, a ring made in each succeeding row or round can link into this loop as if it were a picot. When the ring is drawn up it is attached to, and balanced on this thread, on which it can move. Figure 92 shows such an arrangement: the upper row is made first, the lower follows it, joining its rings when half worked into the space of thread above it. (This formation was used by Riego for deep borders, and described as 'Mignonette' which also means a kind of lace. Her rings were larger and joined to one another by rather long picots.)

Rows so worked can be pulled round into a circle, and any number of concentric rounds added, which for perfect shaping must each start with a new thread. The star-shaped circle shown is built up in this manner. The formation of the actual centre is optional, but in the example there is a central ring carrying fifteen picots: to these are united the fifteen small rings of the first round in the normal way. A measured space of thread is left between the rings. Four subsequent rounds have been worked, with spaces of increasing size, the small rings linking into the spaces of the previous round. In the final one, three Josephine rings provide ornament and give weight and balance to the tips.

Large mats, oval or round, can be made on this principle: they are not difficult to work, but tedious as the measurements should be very accurate. Starching improves the mat when laundered: the effect is crisp and attractive.

CROSSING ONE WORKED LINE WITH ANOTHER

This is not strictly traditional tatting since the work is usually perfectly flat: a worked line of ring or chain does not overlap another. An exception is seen in the rare case of a form of 'raised' tatting, practised by both Riego and Lady Hoare, when a row of rings was bunched together so that they overlapped, but each ring was free and not connected to the one above or beneath it. Overlapping (or crossing) one line with another can, however, be used to greater advantage and produce some interesting effects if the lines are united at the point of intersection. When a line crosses another to meet and unite with a picot, it does so either above or below it: there are therefore two forms of joining, overhand and underhand.

To make a flat underhand crossing

Pass *both* threads *underneath* the chain carrying the picot and draw the ball thread upwards through the picot in the normal way. Continue the chain.

To make a flat overhand crossing

The reverse of the underhand: carry both threads *over* the chain and draw the ball thread downwards through the picot.

Two examples of a line crossing and recrossing itself at predetermined points, The Running Scroll and the Cord of Loops, are given in Figure 94, Plate XVI.

The running scroll

A variation of the ordinary scroll can be made by making a chain cross (either over or under) and join into itself as it progresses, to form loops instead of the traditional rings. This 'running scroll' gives the impression of drawing with a pencil, advancing in one continuous flowing line, and is more graceful than the broken, rigid effect of ring alternating with chain.

The finished scroll can appear to be drawn from either direction (the beginning or end of the chain), such effect depending on whether the crossings are over or underhand. In the model, the crossings are overhand, which gives the effect of a line drawn in the same direction as the working. The same result would appear by using underhand crossings, and reversing after making, since the crossing is in reverse on its opposite side. (Such detail is necessary in the making, for example, of two Baroque scrolls, one the mirror image of the other.)

Start a chain, working (for example) 20 doubles: make a small picot. Work another 20 doubles. The piece is kept the same way up throughout (unlike the ordinary scroll) as the stitches always face outwards. Now curve round the last-made section to meet the picot, and make an overhand crossing described above. The enclosure so formed is really a type of mock-ring, and represents the first loop or ring of the scroll. Continue for 20 doubles for the next section of chain; picot; another 20 doubles; curve round and join into the last-made picot as before. In the model, the distance between the picots now becomes progressively smaller.

The cord of loops

In the cord of loops, two lines are united but the join is not flat. The direction of stitches changes at each intersection which gives a distinctive roll to the chain at this point. A straight chain, worked at slight tension, bearing small picots at regular intervals (in the example 10 doubles), is worked for the required length. When a sufficient length has been made, work twice the number of stitches (20 doubles) after the last picot to make the end loop of the cord. The chain, now described as the working chain, is continued, and returns to the point of origin, crossing the straight chain as it reaches each picot and uniting with it. Hold the piece so that you are now prepared to work back towards the beginning (i.e. by forming a hair-pin bend), with the straight chain nearest to you, all stitches facing out. Join into the last-made picot with an underhand crossing, thereby forming the end loop of the cord. Now turn the work over, and continue with the working chain for 10 doubles, stitches facing up. The free part of the straight chain will still be nearest to you, but with stitches facing up or away from you; twist it so that the stitches face down or towards you, and join the working chain into the next picot, underhand crossing as before. This completes the second loop. Continue with these four actions – reversing the work, making the chain, twisting, and joining – until all the picots have been engaged. It will be noted that all the crossings are worked under. They appear to alternate with overhand crossings because the work has been reversed between each loop. All overhand crossings will produce the same effect.

The result is a firm yet elastic cord of loops, somewhat resembling the cable twist in knitting. Although it may sound complicated it is quick and easy to make. Used as an edging it can take any curve and without alteration turn a fair right-angle. Back and front are similar, the two edges are equal, it can be squeezed together so that the loops are nearly circular, or pulled out so that they are more elongated. It can of course carry additional picots for ornament, or for joining at any point. Figure 94 shows the cord, and also a portion of the running scroll.

Crossing a line presents no problem when that line is free-standing, as in the above examples, for the shuttles can be carried above the work, beneath it, or both, as may be indicated. It is also straightforward when the crossings in a piece (though not free-standing) are either all passing over, or all under, as the shuttles will remain on one side or the other. (To make all underhand crossings, turn the work over and work all on the reverse side, treating as overhand.)

When, however, the line is in the form of a ring, and both types of intersection are required, e.g. passing into the ring and out again, the ring must either be large enough to allow the shuttles to pass through it (which is unlikely) or drawing-up must be postponed until all the joins – possibly several in the same ring – are completed. It is therefore easier to work with chains, i.e. mock-rings, whose ends can be joined later. Passing both over and under the same closed line is shown in Figure 95, which gives two examples of what might be called 'double intersections': four interlinked chains and the emblem of the Olympic Games.

Here there are four chains (two black and two white) of equal length, arranged round a common centre. Each interlinks with its adjacent neighbours, thereby carrying four intersections, the black chains lying above the white at the centre, and beneath them towards the edge. Each chain starts with a small picot, into which the threads are tied on completion. The chain can be manipulated into any shape after joining: in the example one is a full circle, two are heart-shaped, and one has not yet been joined. The work can start with any of the chains, which can be made in any order: in the model the two white were made first, thus carrying all the picots (four each), and the blacks followed, linking them together. Alternatively they can be made in series, in either direction.

PLATE XV THE DAISY MAT (*page* 91)

PLATE XVI SPECIAL ARRANGEMENTS OF STITCHES (*page* 92)
The reversing chain shown in a SCALLOP, Figure 91 (*page* 92) · Mignonette stitch shown in a STRAIGHT PIECE, Figure 92 (*page* 93) · Mignonette stitch shown in a circular MAT, Figure 93 (*page* 93) · Crossing one line with another shown in: The RUNNING SCROLL and CORD OF LOOPS, Figure 94 (*pages* 94, 95), DOUBLE INTERSECTIONS AND OLYMPIC RINGS, Figure 95 (*pages* 96, 97)

The Olympic rings

This is more difficult. Here three upper rings are interlinked into two lying below them (all are worked as mock-rings, each of 46 doubles, which can be made in any order: the example was worked from right to left). The four intersections in any one ring lie within less than its semicircle, which gives the whole an appearance of lightness and movement. 'Over' and 'under' are in a definite sequence and always alternate. This piece is mainly of theoretical interest, and is offered as an example of rather more complicated intersections as they are placed very near together. The difficulty lies not so much in the intersections themselves, but in the added difficulty of keeping the chains circular. Fine thread (70) was used for the model as a coarse one exaggerates the distortion caused by the crossings. It is shown, together with the interlinked chains, in Figure 95, Plate XVI.

For the knotting enthusiasts, plaits and traditional ornamental knots can be portrayed in the flat by using a needle instead of the shuttle, which allows the threads to pass through enclosures already formed by previous intersections.

THE NODE STITCH

As far as I have been able to ascertain, this particular formation has not been previously used. It is the result of a combination of two twists (see Fig. 51). It can make both rings and chains, which have a stiff, corded appearance, bearing small nodes alternately on both sides of the line. One of its features is its ability to replace the nodes with picots.

The description of the composition of the stitch sounds complicated. In practice it is simple enough to make, without necessarily understanding its actual construction, and readers can, if they wish, turn immediately to the paragraph giving directions for working.

The composition of node stitch

In the ordinary line of tatted stitches, as shown in the section on the Tatting Knot, the running thread lies nearest to you, and the stitches rest upon it, facing up. This description depends of course on the particular angle at which you hold your hands, but it indicates the way the threads lie under the thumb.

When you are making a twist, clockwise or anti-clockwise, it does not matter how you hold the threads under the thumb, as the running thread finds its own balance *on the top* of the second thread, occupying a third dimension, in, as it were, a neutral position. The running thread stays straight as an internal core, and the stitches twist round it. When pulled up tightly the completed chain has no defined back, front, or sides: it is the same all the way round. Picots made on such a chain would appear at random in any plane.

In node stitch the running thread also finds its own balance on the top of the chain, but it is worked into the surface, not as an internal core. This is because the chain is rolled one-quarter-way over from under the thumb – it will pull itself into this position – so that what was originally the lower edge is now on the top, and the face of the stitches which in the normal chain lie along the upper edge has now rolled over to lie directly underneath. The stitches stay permanently in this position because you are not making one continual twist, but a series of very short twists in alternate directions which counterbalance one another. No overall twist is generated, as each short turn is compensated immediately by the next one: the chain stays straight.

On the top surface, the chain appears as a firm stitched cord or ridge. The under surface has a notched or corrugated appearance: each notch is the junction of two twists, a right and a left. These junctions are just visible from above, showing alternately on both sides from underneath the line, as very small excrescences or nodes. Hence the suggested name for the stitch, which can produce both rings and chains that are neat, rather narrow in outline, and very firm, with both sides alike.

Because the 'face' of the stitches is now directly underneath and the running thread above in 'neutral', picots, which are actually formed underneath, at the origin of the nodes, can be directed to lie on either side – appearing above or below the line, depending on the type of succeeding twist – clockwise or anti-clockwise.

Directions for working: type of stitch and pattern formulae

Since node stitch is a twist composition, the stitches are described as singles, and since the two halves of the double stitch have different functions it is necessary to name them. It is suggested they be called Plain and Purl respectively, one being the reverse of the other, as in knitting.

Abbreviations: pl=plain, pu=purl, P=picot.

To make the pattern as clear and brief as possible, it is written as a formula, using a bracket to denote the repetition as in arithmetic, the figure placed immediately before the bracket indicating the number of times the enclosure is to be repeated.

A chain in node stitch

On a continuous thread make a holding knot as for an ordinary chain. Work three plain stitches and then three purl. This constitutes the repetition.

After a few stitches you will feel the pull of the running thread, and feel that the work has twisted slightly from under the thumb. For convenience adjust the thumb so that the pull is a direct one, with the thread on the top of the work. As you proceed (tightly) with the 3pl, 3pu, small nodes will appear, equally spaced on both sides of the chain; each occurs at the junction of the two twists, where their direction alters. A chain of 10 repetitions will give 10 nodes along the upper edge, and 9 on the lower, since you cannot start or end with one. Written as a formula, such an arrangement would be: 10(3pl 3pu).

To make picots (of any length), leave a space of thread at the junction of the twist, i.e. between the two types of stitches. Instead of the node a picot will be formed. As with all picots, they are formed by the stitch following them, not preceding; plain stitches produce (or succeed) picots facing down, purl stitches make them face upwards. This is all you need to memorize: *Plain Drops Down; Purl Stands Skywards.*

A chain of 10 repetitions with picots facing up for the first half of its length, and down for the second half, would be written as follows: 5(3pl P 3pu) 5(P 3pl 3pu). Picots on both sides would be: 10(3pl P 3pu P).

This last could be written in several ways: if as above, it must be accompanied by the statement 'omitting the last picot in the last repetition', although of course the picot could not exist if it is at the end of a line. In this case, and more accurately, it should be written: 9(3pl P 3pu P) 3pl P 3pu, which gives the last group (not quite a full repetition) correctly. Figure 96, Plate XVII, shows a chain, the first part consisting of nodes only – 10(3pl 3pu); followed by a section of 5 picots (this time facing down) and another 5 facing up: finally, graduated picots on both sides.

In the description of the stitch, three single stitches have been used for each twist, but even with only two the node will form, making a very compact chain (or ring) with nodes very close together. Three is the most suitable number, but four and possibly more can be used, provided the chain does not start twisting on itself, which it will do as soon as there are too many stitches.

Since node stitch cannot be worked on the reverse side, it is an advantage to be able to make the picot above or below with equal facility. For example, if the pattern shows two parallel chains (which must be started from the same direction) with picots facing towards one another (or outwards) one chain is then the mirror image of the other, i.e. they make a pair, right and left. Therefore on one side the picots will be worked above the line, and on the other below.

Rings carrying picots inside are much easier to make by the node stitch than in pearl tatting, which also features them, as there is no additional thread to handle.

Some applications of node stitch

The reverse side of the work can be used as a decorative line (or ring) when it is composed of nodes only. Rows of picots seen from underneath give a somewhat smudged effect, unless they are very long.

A ring carried above a chain can be turned inside out before drawing up, if the reverse side is to be shown. Make it, turn it and press the stitches together neatly, to be sure that none capsize, before drawing up.

Rings on both sides of the chain

An important feature of node stitch is that, since the running thread always remains on top, in its neutral position, the second thread can, instead of making a picot, leave the chain *on either side* to make independent ornamental rings, returning to the chain to resume its function. The running thread maintains its unbroken tension throughout, and the sequence of plain and purl is undisturbed. It is, however, not quite as simple as it appears, as the rings must satisfy three conditions:

1. Their required position (i.e. above or below the line).
2. On drawing-up, the running thread must be on the right-hand side, as you are working from left to right.
3. The upper surface must remain so, and they can only be worked right side up.

To make the upper rings is straightforward; worked normally they satisfy all three conditions. The lower, which are the mirror images of the upper, are deceptive. There are three possible ways of manipulating them wrongly, having made them correctly, as you will discover on experimenting. The correct way would be to work them left-handed, which would fulfil all three conditions, but since you are unlikely to do this, the only solution is to make them as if they were to lie above, and then turn them inside out. This will bring them right side up, below the line, the thread on the right, ready for incorporation in the chain. You are in fact performing two inversions – inside out, and upside down, which together give the correct position.

Node stitch in combination with the normal chain

A very short portion of node stitch – only two stitches – can be introduced into an ordinary chain, in order to produce a single picot on the opposite side; this is of great value in some designs. After a normal double stitch, ending with a purl, work one more purl; keeping the thread on the top, form the picot with one plain, and resume the chain with one plain, one purl, i.e. the normal double stitch. The chain is thus interrupted only very slightly, the diversion is almost unnoticeable in fine thread, and the picot lies below. This picot can be used for joining to other parts of the work which are made later. Figure 97 shows a chain bearing assorted rings on both sides at regular intervals. The first ring lies above, of 2pl, 2pu, nodes only. The next lies below, with outside picots at every node, inside picots at alternate nodes. The third, facing up, carries inside picots at every node, and one outside picot only, at its apex. Finally a short section of a normal chain carrying two picots on the under side. (Plate XVII.)

It is suggested that the beginner first confines herself to chains, which are very easy and quick to make; progressing to independent rings with variously disposed picots, and finally to rings carried below a chain.

MULTIPLE DEAD ENDS

A blind or dead end (without ends of threads) is automatically produced when starting a chain on a continuous thread. (The word 'end' here applies to the beginning, not the terminal.) It must have occurred to some workers that it would be an advantage if one pair of threads could produce several such ends in the same motif, without adding threads for each new beginning.

Multiple dead ends can be made by forming a number of false chains with either of the threads of a continuous pair. The false chains are 'thrown out' into space at any point and return the thread to the same point.

The 'false' chain died a natural death as soon as the true chain superseded it; no one seems to have considered it worth development, although it offered a constructional advantage which nothing else can. It has here been revived in a Seven-branched Candlestick, which is composed of a central upright (chain) carrying lateral branches. These are worked on the same principle as the Bunch of Grapes (Plate III), the branches being thrown out as the leaves and stalk are thrown out from the grape stem.

In the candlestick, the central candle is made first, on a continuous thread starting with a picot. The first part is a twist (Fig. 51). The chain is continued to the first pair of branches. A *single* thread is used for each branch: the running thread of the central chain forms those on the left side, the second thread those on the right: thus they do not cross one another.

At a suitably measured distance from the main stem, a holding knot is made and a false chain is worked back to the stem. The thread on the shuttle side of the knot makes the stitches, using the measured distance as the running thread: when the stem is reached, the branch on the other side is made with the other thread, in the same manner. Both threads are now together again, and the stem continued as an ordinary chain. The whole candelabra is therefore worked on one pair. In the illustration the work has been turned over so that the running thread of the stem is lying on the right-hand side (Fig. 98, Plate XVII).

PEARL AND RAISED TATTING (Figs. 99–102, Plate XVII)

In her books, *The Pearl Tatting Book* (1867) and *The Raised Tatting Book* (1868), Mlle Riego describes the simultaneous use of one (and also two) extra threads when making a chain. As this method is now obsolete, and no subsequent writer appears to have developed it, only brief descriptions are given. Nevertheless it opens up a new field which would be well worth investigation, and once the rhythm is established is not as difficult as it looks.

'Pearl tatting' consists of chains called 'Pearl Beading'. To make such a chain, a third thread with which to form stitches is used, in addition to the normal one, but the same running thread is used for both, alternately. The stitches from the two threads face in opposite directions, so that the result looks very much like picots on both sides of a chain (Fig. 54), but is actually much firmer and flatter. The picots or 'pearls' which appear (on both sides) do so spontaneously when the running thread is pulled up. If longer loops are required, then extra thread is allowed for them as in an ordinary picot.

Rings are also possible. The extra thread is worked in alternately with the loop round the hand. Where some additional ornament is required, such as a small ring, it can be made on the extra thread (provided it is on a shuttle) at any point, as it is independent of the running thread supporting the ring. The two rings shown in Figure 100 are worked identically, on a white thread. The extra thread is black, and carries the ornament. One of the rings is turned inside out so that the ornament faces in the opposite direction. Since an equal number of stitches are facing both ways, there is no distinction between 'outside' and 'inside' – it can be pulled up to face either way.

Raised tatting

This is simply a development of pearl. When a second extra thread is used (the shuttle therefore working on three threads in rotation) the result is called 'Raised' tatting. presumably because on one side there will now be two rows of picots, one overlapping the other. One set can lie above the other, or they can be intertwined, according to the position of the threads when working. (The title 'raised tatting' is also applied by Riego to another formation, but it appears to describe only the overlapping of concentric rings of increasing size.)

In Figure 101, the picots on the 'single' side are short, those on the double side are both longer, one more so. One row lies above the other. One double stitch only (forming the picot) is made on each thread on the double side.

In Figure 102, the single side is short, as above: on the double side they are both long (equal) and they intertwine. The number of stitches allotted to each thread is double that of the first example, i.e. two.

To obtain a 'natural' curve more stitches must be worked on one side. If the stitches are equal on both sides, the result will be a straight line. In the examples they are equal: tension has controlled shape, for by leaving the tension loose the piece can be pulled into a curve in either direction – but logically with the larger picots on the outside.

It would seem that a further study in the use of the extra threads would be worth considering. The opportunities they present are at once apparent to those interested in experiment. Riego shows several patterns, chiefly edgings and rectangular pieces, incorporating these pearl beadings, which are shaped into scallops, drawn into circular forms, and generally exploited to advantage.

The next two figures (quatrefoil and coronet) may at first sight appear to be examples of multiple dead ends and the long space of thread, but in fact they are not, as both are worked by ordinary methods.

The quatrefoil (with open centre)

This is really two scrolls, an outer surrounding the inner, which is the quatrefoil proper. Its rings are very small, and the four chains deeply curved (tight tension); they unite a short distance from each ring, thus thrusting it forward to make a blunt rigid point (the cusp). The piece is begun with one of the rings, to which the fourth chain is eventually joined. In the outer scroll, which forms the surrounding circle, the four rings are large, and the chains are very flat (loose tension); both rings and chains are joined to the inner scroll (the ring twice, the chain once). If worked at correct tension, and stretched on a board, the piece will hold its shape (Fig. 103).

The coronet

In the little coronet there are long spaces of thread between the Josephine rings which ornament the five peaks, but no ring is worked *into* a space, which is the essence of Figure 92. The piece is worked mainly on one thread. A band of five joined Josephine rings is made and the thread then brought back over the band, into which it joins, carrying five spaced Josephine rings: sufficient thread has been left at the beginning to form the short chain which is then worked to lie along the upper edge of the band (Fig. 104, Plate XVII).

CHAPTER VI

Working with Multiple Threads

FOR special effects, and often in free-style tatting, more than one thread can be used in either or both shuttles. The extra thread(s) need not be of the same thickness as the first. It may be of another material, of the same or in a contrasting colour. Multiple threads are not very suitable for large rings if the threads are coarse: they are better adapted to chains, which, however, lose their natural curve and tend to straighten. If a second thread is added to the right-hand shuttle when making a chain, the colour of course will not show, and the resultant chain will be thicker than normal, but not so thick as when it is added to the second shuttle. Here the new colour will be apparent. Striking blends of colour can be achieved in this way.

It is not difficult to work with double threads: they are in fact much easier to unpick, should this be necessary. It is important to keep both at the same tension, and if picots are made, to see that both loops are of equal length. The continuous thread method is of particular advantage when using multiple threads as the number of ends is reduced by half, a consideration if there are several in both shuttles.

Combining threads of different materials

'The numerous purposes for which the work can be applied far exceeds the limits of this book as it admits of being made in every material', announced Mlle Riego in her preface to *Golden Stars in Tatting and Crochet* (1861). This lead, given exactly a hundred years ago, has been followed by very few designers. Considering the number of materials there now are, both natural and synthetic, this ambitious claim has even more to recommend it than in her own day. Some at least might be tried in the making of purely decorative pieces. A fine (coloured) sewing cotton in the right-hand shuttle, producing small rings with large picots, can give good effects when combined with the ordinary cotton in the second shuttle for making the chains in which it forms the running thread. The sewing cotton makes the stitches, strengthened by the stronger thread which carries them. Real silk can be used in the same manner.

Metallic threads (which fracture easily) are best worked over cotton or silk threads, preferably of a near-colour, as chains: they can make rings, but very small ones. If a larger ring is needed, make a mock-ring. A suitable design worked in gold or silver makes an attractive piece of pin-on 'jewellery'. Great care is necessary when transposing the knot – it must have plenty of room in which to turn. (The first half of the stitch is especially difficult to turn over and must be made at a considerable distance from the previous stitch.) On no account must the thread be bent at a sharp angle, or dragged across itself. Once turned, the stitch can be pushed up tightly into place. Double metallic threads are quite successful and have been used in the pattern given for the Dragon-fly.

The use of gold thread is earlier than might be supposed: Riego was possibly using real gold in the material she called gold 'twist' or 'twine', for her soutache of crochet on her embroidered waistcoat, and for her tatted golden 'stars', which were four small rings drawn into a circle, incorporated in medallions worked in coloured silks. They are circular, square and hexagonal, and very primitive in design, consisting mainly of small motifs joined together in rows, i.e. with no defined centre. They were suggested as trimming for sleeves and cuffs, arranged to form bands which were sewn on to the material.

PATTERN FOR QUEEN ANNE'S LACE

This pattern, inspired by one of the many varieties of Cow Parsley, is offered as an introduction to a flower produced in tatting.

Making a flower piece is a form of drawing – your drawing. The exact number of stitches used in the model are only a guide: the example is not intended to be copied stitch by stitch, but is given rather as a demonstration of what a few basic motifs can be made to do, and how to assemble them to produce a particular effect. The piece is not an elementary one, and requires a delicacy of balance of the fingers. The rings for the flowers are very small and almost all identical. The chains are more complicated: they are both single and multiple, forming the stalks, and some are 'led' or worked into the main central stem, which therefore becomes thicker towards the base. For a first attempt this is not recommended, and it is suggested that the stalks from the flowers and leaves are made to the required length and then tied and cut, the ends sewn into position on the mount, tucked out of sight, behind the stem. This is much easier. The reason for leading them in is that if you want to make the stalk thicker towards the base, as it should be, it is reasonable to use the threads that are already in position: when you are proficient in handling multiple chains, then they can be incorporated.

The size of the thread is optional: the piece can be worked all in one colour, in thread of the same thickness, or there can be variation in both. The model is worked in cottons No. 20 and 70, in white, and shades of green, brown, grey and cream, home-dyed.

A spray of the plant includes flowers, seeds and leaves, with individual stalks and a main stem which bears the top-most motif. In nature the plant is very stiff: the whole appearance is one of rigidity but also of grace and lightness. To emulate this the curvature of the stalks is very slight: they leave the stem at a sharp angle. The incoming stalks are arranged in 'whorls', i.e. circles round the stem (not alternating up it). This is an important botanical feature of the plant, and should be observed in its representation. From a constructional point of view the piece demonstrates, besides the multiple chains, the principle of the paired motif, which occurs frequently in flower and leaf patterns. When two similar motifs lie side by side, or across a line, they are worked on the same pair of threads, the second in the reverse order of the first: by so doing it is possible to reduce the number of ends of threads, which is the first consideration of the designer.

To make the full flower (Cotton No. 70, one shuttle)

This is made in two parts, an independent central medallion of six repetitions, and an outer border, which is not attached to it but sewn into position on the mount.

Central medallion: a circle of rings is surrounded by and joined to six identical circles. All the rings are the same, of eight doubles carrying seven small unmeasured picots. Make one ring, which will be the centre: make another, as close as possible: make a third, joining at its first picot (i.e. where its first picot would otherwise be) to the last picot of the ring last made, in the manner of Figure 37, but do not make long picots for the join at the rings should lie very compactly. Continue for a total of six rings round the centre one, joining always to the ring last made, and finally the last to the first. Twice during the round pass the thread through a picot on the centre ring, in the manner of the daisy. Pull up all the rings very tightly. After the last ring,

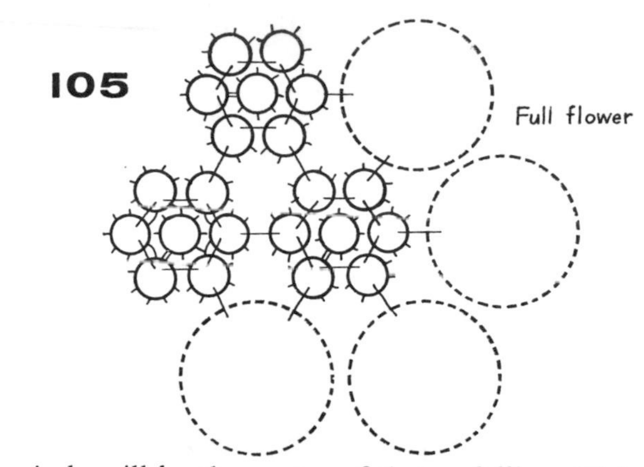

tie and cut. This circle will be the centre of the medallion. Make six more identical circles, joining each as you work, once to the central circle, and to the circle last made: join the last circle to the first. This completes the central medallion, which could serve as a small flower by itself. If required to be larger, add the outer border. Figure 105 shows the relative positions of the circles, and the positions of the joined rings.

The outer border: This consists of ten circles, made in the same manner, and joined in series, but with no centre one. In the example the rings are slightly larger, ten double stitches carrying nine picots. As they are larger, ten circles are sufficient to surround the central medallion which it over- and under-laps slightly: but if the work is required to be perfectly flat and symmetrical, twelve will be necessary and of the same size as those in the medallion itself: in this case it should be joined to it. Otherwise the medallion and border will be assembled on the mount and both sewn into position.

To make the flower-in-section (Cotton No. 70 on a continuous thread)

This is worked in two parts: easier than it appears. There are several ways of achieving this umbrella-like formation of short radiating stalks supporting a 'frill' of flowers, giving the effect of a bunch of individual flowerets. The following method gives the minimum number of free ends.

With a continuous thread make a ring of six doubles carrying five very small picots (the stalk ring). From this ring five spokes will radiate, and the stalk will also be joined to it. If you are making the pattern all in one thickness, the threads from this ring can now be continued into a chain for the stalk. If not, proceed to make one of the spokes with these threads.

Make a short chain of about ten doubles (according to the length you think appropriate) – the younger the flower the shorter the chains, and also the less spread apart on the mount. (In the model the upper flower has fifteen doubles, the lower has ten.) At the end of the chain make a ring of three measured picots (four doubles). Their length is again optional. In the upper flower they are all equal: length $\frac{3}{4}$ inch (or 2 centimetres) before drawing up. In the lower, the centre picot is slightly less than this, and those on either side less still. Draw up the ring very tightly. Cut off the threads. These ends will be used for sewing on to the mount, so leave them long enough to thread with a needle. *This applies to all the ends in the pattern.*

You have four more spokes to make: these will be made in pairs (the paired motif), the first of each pair starting with its ring, the second ending with it: therefore only one will carry free ends.

With a new continuous thread (as the length of chain is so short it is not worth threading two shuttles: leave a length of thread of about eighteen inches for working the chain), make a ring of three measured picots, as above; work a short chain as before and link into the picot on the stalk-ring lying next to the spoke last made; make a locking stitch to break the tension; link into the next picot on the stalk ring; make another spoke of chain and ring; tie and cut as before. Figure 106 shows the stalk ring, the first spoke, and the next pair of spokes: the size of the picots is exaggerated.

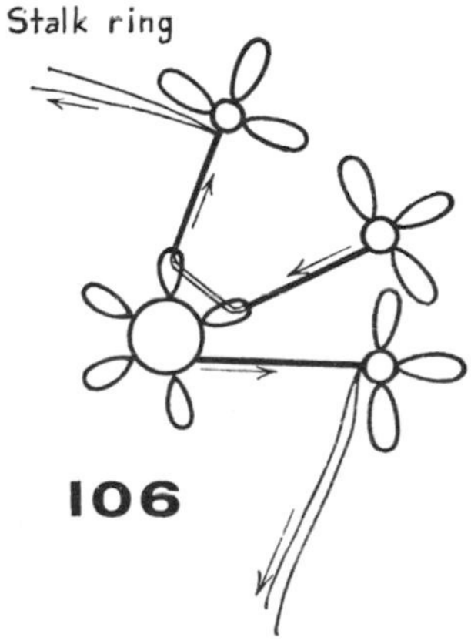

Flower in section:
Stalk ring

106

Repeat with another pair for the next two picots: this completes the five spokes. The remaining picot is for attachment for the stalk. If you have already made the stalk, the fifth picot will be free: work a single spoke on to it. When the spokes are completed, slip a short length of coarse thread through the stalk picot (if vacant) and make one stitch: this gives a temporary handle for the flower and is a help when trying on the mount to estimate the length of stalk you need.

The frill of rings: There are two ways of attaching the frill. A string of rings may be worked first, and then worked on to the picots of the spokes with another pair of threads: or the string can be composed directly on to them, linking into the picots as you work. The essential aim is to avoid too smooth a line: it tends to become a perfect half-circle. It should be slightly scalloped to give the impression of individual flowerets: to assist in this effect the picots were of two lengths in the second flower. In either method, the ring is the same as in the central medallion of the full flower, i.e. eight doubles carrying seven picots. One ring for each picot, i.e. fifteen rings.

In the upper flower a string was worked first: three rings joined closely together (which draw them into a slight curve): a short space of thread, and then another three, not joined to the first triplet. To attach, use a continuous thread, either on a shuttle with a long free end, or substitute a needle for the shuttle. Work the string of rings into position, making the tatting stitch correctly to pick up the picots, not a sewing stitch, linking the thread into any convenient part of the string. Leave spaces of thread where appropriate. Very few stitches are necessary, just enough to disguise the passage of the new thread. At the end, tie and cut, and use the free ends for sewing on the mount. In the model of the upper flower, two extra triplets of flowers were worked and sewn into position to make the string a little thicker at these points: this is optional.

In the lower flower the string was worked directly on to the picots, and no space of thread left between: all the rings are joined together, by slightly longer picots. The final result is very similar to the first and it is a matter of choice as to which method you prefer – the even picots with the applied frill, or uneven and worked-on frill: use the one which you can work the fastest and with which you can best produce the slight scallop.

The head of seeds

A head of seeds is composed of several seed clusters: the example carries three. Each cluster consists of the cluster ring, to which individual seeds are attached, and is joined by a short chain to a 'stalk ring' which is made in one with the stalk. The cluster ring is made first.

With one shuttle: make a ring of six doubles carrying five picots (the number is optional) leaving about 18 inches of thread before starting the ring. Pull up tightly. At a distance of about $\frac{1}{2}$ inch (more or less) from the cluster ring, make a seed ring of eight doubles with a small picot at its centre: pull up, cut off the shuttle and draw the free end of thread straight through the picot, so that the thread lies up the centre of the ring. Cut off, leaving about $\frac{1}{8}$ inch, and untwist it slightly with the fingers: this gives an almost exact representation of the seed carrier. This completes one seed. Thread the 18-inch length with a needle and make another seed, about $\frac{1}{2}$ inch away, as before. The cluster ring has now two seeds, as shown in Figure 107.

To make the second and subsequent pairs of seeds: start with a seed ring: link into a picot on the cluster ring, leaving the ½-inch space of thread: make the seed ring for the second of the pair. At the base of each ring there will be the free end, from the start and the finish: draw these ends through their picots as before. Continue with similar pairs, one pair for each picot, leaving one free for stalk attachment. The clusters will be connected together later.

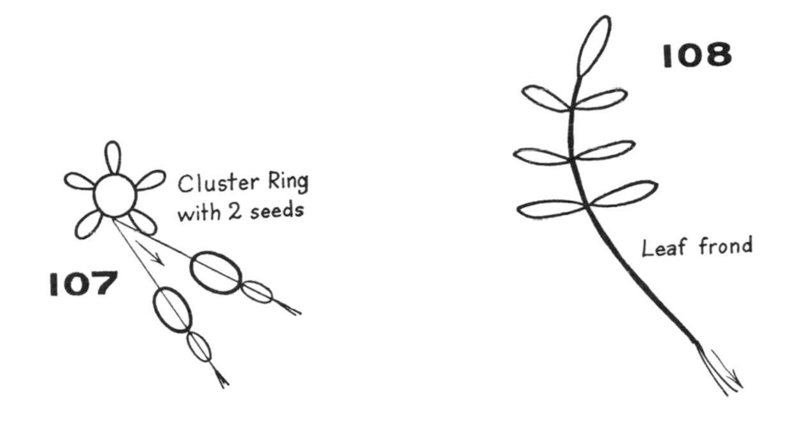

The leaf (Cottons 20 and 70)

The leaf is simply a modified Figure 54, picots on both sides of a chain. The picots are arranged in pairs (one on either side of the chain, close together: they gradually increase in size, and also the sections of chain separating them.

Start with a picot at the head of a chain: work about three doubles: make a long picot, reverse the chain and make another picot of about the same length: work three or four doubles: another pair of slightly longer picots: continue for three or four pairs. This constitutes a 'frond', which will be the top-most extremity of the leaf. Continue with the chain for as long as necessary: this will be the central stalk of the leaf. Crossing the stalk below the top frond are pairs of additional fronds, made like the first, but each pair slightly larger than the one before it. The first of each pair will start like the top frond, with a picot at the head of a chain: when its stalk is long enough work across the main stem, either gripping it tightly in its passage, or into a small picot left for the purpose. Then work the second of the pair, the reverse of the first, ending with the double stitch which forms the last picot, which pull into line with the chain. Work one or more sprays of fronds on to the central stalk of the leaf. These sprays of fronds, which are described as composite leaves, are quick to make, the picots are made by eye and a few discrepancies do not matter. The top and upper fronds can be made in finer thread, or the whole can be of one thickness. This principle of assembly can be carried out indefinitely, using a complete spray as a top-most frond, and working pairs of sprays to cross it. When mounted, the fronds can be set at any angle, or if preferred they can be pulled over so that all lie on one side of the central leaf-stalk. This leaf is highly stylized, and cannot claim to be a faithful representation of the plant in question.

The main stem and stalks

If you are 'leading in' the stalks from the flowers, they must be made first, and the main stem last. Otherwise make the main stem first, thus setting the overall height of the spray. All the flowers described above are ready to receive their stalks except the head of seeds: each cluster still requires a short chain to connect it to the focal point of the 'head', a ring not yet made: this is incorporated in the stalk.

To complete the head of seeds

First make the stalk ring: if you are using a single pair of threads make a ring with as many (very small) picots as you have seed clusters. If double threads, as in the model, make the ring of four double stitches without picots: these are looser and a thread can be inserted directly into a thread on the ring, making it more compact. In either case, after the ring is drawn up, continue with a chain for the stalk of the required length to meet the main stem. Tie and cut, or leave the threads for incorporation.

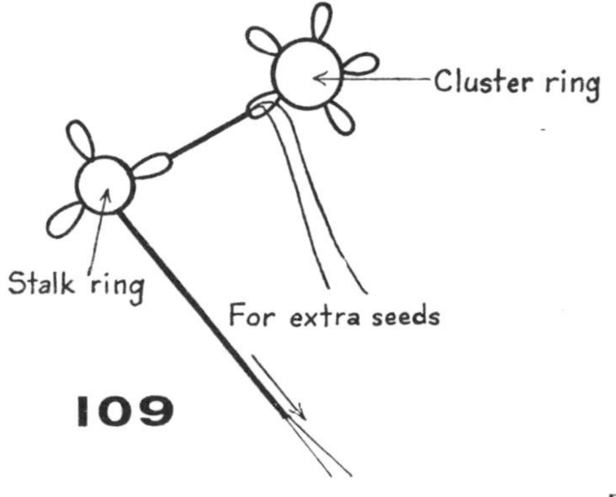

With a continuous thread, link into a picot on the stalk ring: work a short chain of about fifteen doubles: link into the free picot on the cluster ring. The ends of both threads can be used to form extra seeds, thus disposing of them to advantage instead of merely cutting them off. After making a locking stitch on the picot, thread the

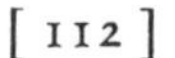

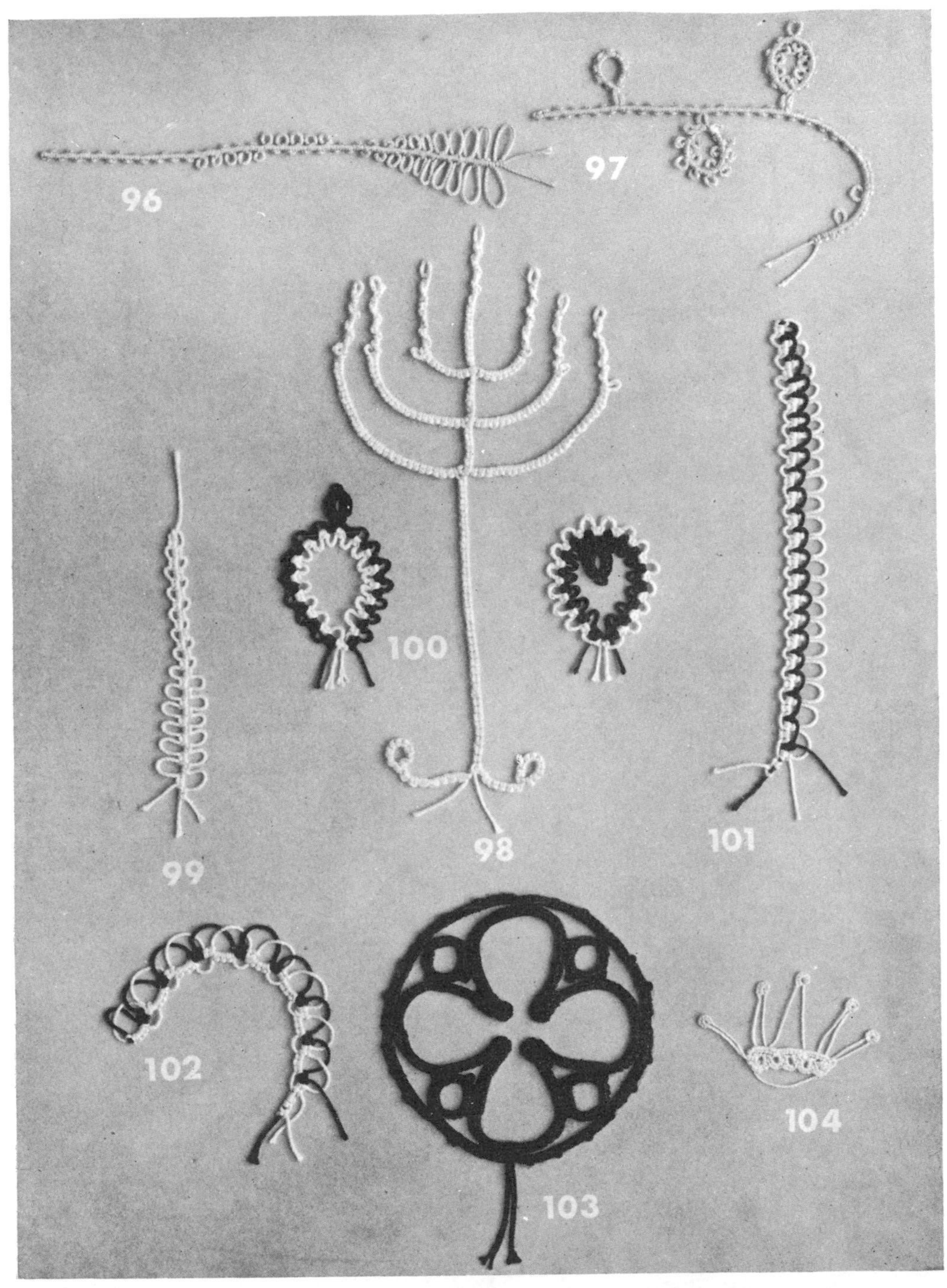

PLATE XVII SPECIAL ARRANGEMENTS OF STITCHES

A CHAIN in node stitch, Figure 96 (*page* 99) · RINGS ON A CHAIN in node stitch, Figure 97 (*page* 101) SEVEN-BRANCHED CANDLESTICK (dead ends), Figure 98 (*page* 102) · A CHAIN of pearl beading, Figure 99 (*page* 102) · TWO RINGS in pearl tatting, Figure 100 (*page* 102) · A CHAIN in raised tatting, Figure 101 (overlapping) (*page* 103) · A CHAIN in raised tatting, Figure 102 (intertwining) (*page* 103) · A QUATREFOIL, Figure 103 (*page* 103) · A CORONET, Figure 104 (*page* 104)

PLATE XVIII QUEEN ANNE'S LACE AND DRAGON-FLY (*page* 114)

two ends with a needle (separately) and make the seeds as previously described. If you have more than three seed clusters, make more picots on the stalk ring, but a ring of double threads can be stretched to take almost any number.

The flower stalks

For the full flower, make an ordinary chain of single or double threads of the required length, tie and cut. The end is concealed on the mount under the edge of the flower, not joined to it. If the stalks of the flower sections are not already made, work an ordinary chain of single or double threads, starting by linking into the free picot on the stalk ring. If you are using double threads, link into the ring itself, disregarding the picot which will be too small.

The main stem

In the model the top-most motif is a flower section. It could of course have been any other motif (except a leaf). With a continuous thread (single or double) join on to the flower in the manner described above and continue for the entire length of the main stem: if you are leading in, incorporate some of the threads from the other stalks (all would be too many). Otherwise, proceed with an unbroken chain to the base. Tie and cut.

MOUNTING

So far you have only exhibited technique in making: assembly requires some artistic ability. Mounting is not done in a hurry: the finished effect is as important as the making of the motifs. Having prepared the mount, lay the pieces in position, using the free ends of thread where they occur to sew them down by threading each with a needle and carrying it to the under side: if you need any additional stitches, use a fine sewing cotton of matching colour. Use as few and as small stitches as possible: leave the seeds to fall freely. A stalk made of a thick multiple thread may be turned over so that the stitches are facing underneath, instead of lying on their side. This gives a narrow smoother line, equal on both sides. In nature, stalks whether round, flat or square are the same on all sides. The chain of course is not. Do not cut off the ends at the back until you are satisfied with the effect you want. The stalks of the incoming flowers and leaves can be shortened by undoing a few stitches if necessary. This is not the easiest of flowers to assemble, on account of its botanical form: it is much simpler to place flower stalks on alternate sides of a curving stem. Still easier is to make a number of independent flowers, one to a stalk and then arrange them as a bunch, partly overlapping one another. The complete spray, with a dragon-fly, is shown in Plate XVIII.

THE DRAGON-FLY

The dragon-fly is included as an example of working in metallic thread. It should not be your first piece in this medium, and to become familiar with the pattern make some practice flies first in stiff linen thread if possible, otherwise thick black cotton. These practice pieces can be used to decorate a lampshade.

The anatomy of an insect must be correctly reproduced if it is to appear convincing. All insects are composed of three main parts, the head, thorax and abdomen, whose relative sizes vary according to the species. In the order Anisoptera the head is the smallest of these organs, with large eyes: it does not carry visible antennae as many insects do. The thorax is short and thick with two pairs of wings on the upper surface, three pairs of legs beneath. The abdomen is thin, long and supple: in this case with a pair of pincers at the terminal. This much basic anatomy must be observed: legs cannot emerge spontaneously from the abdomen as they do in some embroidered specimens.

There is more than one method of making the thorax: to be correct the wings should be carried on a dead-centre line, and the right and left of a pair must be opposite one another: it is impossible to satisfy both these conditions. To ensure the former, the wings cannot be in exact alignment: to make them so they must be carried on both sides of a mock-ring: in which case they are not centrally placed, for a view of laterally extended wings.

In the method suggested the head is a ring on a single thread: the thorax is a mock-ring carrying three measured picots on each side (for two pairs of wings and legs): the abdomen is on double threads, linked into a picot at the base of the thorax, and divided into two separate chains for the pincers at the terminal.

To make the head

Wind a shuttle with gold thread and at about 24 inches from the free end, make a ring of six doubles, working rather loosely, with two fairly large picots for the eyes, equally spaced, two doubles apart. These picots will be pulled out afterwards which will help to tighten the ring.

The thorax

With the same threads, make a chain for the mock-ring: one double: three measured picots $2\frac{1}{2}$ inches in length before drawing up: a small picot: repeat the three measured picots (the last double is the one which forms the last picot). The chain is now equally balanced on both sides of the small picot. Make sure the long picots are all lying correctly before tightening: they tend to slip over owing to their weight, and pull the chain out of line. Link into the start of the chain at the base of the head, pulling the head and thorax slightly apart – the junction is a loose one. Tie the threads together and cut off leaving about 3 inches on both. These two ends will be the foremost pair of legs which are carried in front of the wings, near the head. Figure 110 shows the head and the thorax.

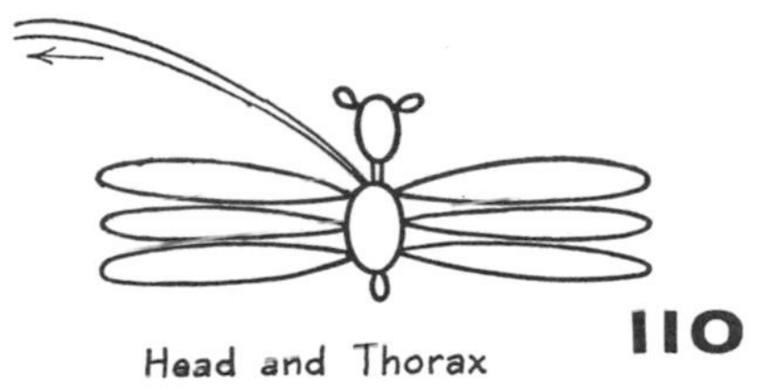

Head and Thorax **110**

The abdomen

Take about 2 yards of thread, bend it in half, and wind the bend on to the shuttle for about 9 inches: you now have a continuous double thread. Link into the small picot at the base of the thorax and make a chain for as long as necessary: this is easy – double metallic threads have no difficulty in turning over. When long enough, cut off the shuttle. The pincers: separate the shuttle threads and with the fingers make two short chains, working respectively on the other two threads: three or four doubles is enough. Leave untied, as the full length of the abdomen can be controlled by pulling on these running threads when adjusting on the mount. If you cannot manage the gold threads on the shuttle – i.e. it continually fractures – use a black cotton instead, as the running thread for the entire piece, making a mock-ring for the head.

The legs

Place the insect upside down and having pulled the picots on both sides carefully and firmly, take the middle pair and tie a knot with them across the centre of the thorax: tie twice, as tightly as possible. Cut through the tips: the result is two pairs of legs. Bend each sharply twice to make acute angles, also the pair near the neck, which are cut to the same length. All will probably have to be trimmed back a little. Pull the upper pair forward and out, the last pair downwards: the middle pair lie under the wings. The knot has a twofold purpose in that it helps to draw the sides of the thorax together and give the effect of a solid thick line. If you are filling the wings, tie the knot but do not cut to form the legs, until the wings are completed.

The wings

The wings alone cannot be shaped more than by pulling them out so that they are equal on both sides of the body. If the thread has not been accidentally twisted in the making of the picots they will make graceful curves as they are. To reproduce more nearly their natural lines, they may be filled with cellophane which holds them in position: it is also an extra adornment. The cellophane should be approximately of the thickness and toughness normally used to cover cartons, etc. It may be crumpled, but not clouded from finger-marks.

A dragon-fly's wings are straight, long and narrow, with slightly rounded tips: the pairs do not overlap, and are not tilted forward as in many other insects.

Filling the wings: The wing-picots, one at a time, are made slightly sticky on the underside with a transparent adhesive. This is best applied with a pin which has been stuck into the neck of the tube and withdrawn. The wing is then pressed into position on the cellophane, which has been crumpled and squeezed between the fingers and then flattened out. (This causes it to catch more light than if quite smooth.) Try to make each member of a pair the same length and width. If you cannot do this by eye, draw the wing on a piece of paper and lay the cellophane over it: this will act as a guide, but it is unlikely that it will be exactly the same size as the picot: establish the width of the wing rather than its length. The adhesive dries almost immediately. The excess cellophane is then cut off very carefully up to the margin of the thread. Do not, by mistake, cut into the other wings or legs when trimming.

If, in conclusion, you have produced the appearance of a neatly made bow tie, rather than organs of flight, it would be better to leave the picots without embellishment.

A side view

A side view of the insect with wings folded together over the back can also be made, and is much easier for filling. The members of each pair will overlap, and the same piece of cellophane can fill both simultaneously. The head is worked as before, but squeezed together after making: the thorax is one straight chain, carrying all the long picots in series: after a locking stitch the threads are continued for the abdomen. As this is a side view, and therefore the chain is thicker in appearance, the addition of a second thread is not necessary. Seen from the side, six legs are too many: two pairs are enough.

Once made, the dragon-fly is very strong and will stand a fair amount of manipulation. If the wings have been correctly filled they should lie straight on the mount without stitching, but a small stitch can be made through the cellophane with a very fine needle and terylene thread. If unfilled, leave them loose. Sew firmly through the thorax and once or twice through the abdomen to keep it lying with the stitches facing downwards, using the thread ends from the pincers, after drawing them through the mount. The wings should curve slightly upwards towards the glass (if the piece is mounted as a picture) which should be raised from the mount by a fillet fitted into the frame.

CHAPTER VII

Finishing the Work

WASHING: Workers whose hands can produce unsoiled tatting, the last picot as fresh as the first, do not have to concern themselves with washing it. Not everyone is so fortunate and usually a large white piece is washed on completion. The best way for doing this is to follow the method used for washing lace, i.e. to tack the work flat, on to a piece of white flannel sewn round a large glass jar. Immerse it in a bowl of warm soap-suds or one of the many other detergents and plunge gently up and down. The bottle may be stood in a saucepan and brought to the boil if the work is very soiled. Boiling will alter the tone of the thread according to the detergent used: as a rule it becomes brighter, loosing its faint cream tone, when compared with the original ball. If the work is very soiled, leave in the hot water for some time. Then take out the bottle and rinse well; take the lace off the flannel and lay it flat in a solution of borax in water which has some bleaching qualities and is also a very slight stiffener. As threads tighten when wet, the whole piece will be rigid and possibly distorted, until dry. After soaking in borax for a short time, remove it and blot between folds of warm white blotting paper, or lay it on a soft towel. (Keep the work flat at all times: do not roll it up when carrying it about, unless it is a long edging, when it can be wrapped round a piece of stiff card.) When nearly dry, pull it into shape with the fingers, and straighten the picots if necessary by pulling them out with a pin.

Pressing: If you do press it, do so lightly on the wrong side with a warm iron between the folds of a damp smooth cloth, or on one of the plastic foam ironing-board covers. Pressing is in order for work which has been applied to fabrics and is in constant use: if it is for exhibition and has been washed, it should not be pressed, but stretched.

Stretching: For this, a flat surface rather larger than the piece of work is needed. It must not be too soft, or the pins will slip, and if too hard it will be very painful putting them in. (Use a thimble.) A cork mat is rather soft: a plain deal board will do, unless it is very seasoned and full of knots in the wood. Compressed paper (the back of a dartboard) is very good. Lay the work, when dry, on the board, and put a rustless pin into each picot, pressing the pin in firmly, the picot at the correct angle. When all the pins are in sprinkle liberally with water, and tilt the board so that the water drains off. Leave to dry; it can be taken off in twenty-four hours or given another sprinkling and left longer: it cannot be overstretched. When taken off the board (and take the pins out carefully) it should be perfectly in shape, and rigid as far as the pattern permits.

Mounting: Mounting includes the sewing of edgings on to the material which it borders, e.g. linen mats, lingerie, handkerchiefs, etc. (and also the mounting of decorative pieces on a prepared background for framing).

The work is attached to the fabric either by its picots, or by a 'space' of thread, whichever the pattern has intended. The sewing thread should not show: it should be very fine and soft, such as embroidery cotton (not stranded). This is obtainable in many colours. Run the needle through the edge of the hem, to appear only at the position where it takes up the picot, which should just touch the material: one stitch through the picot is enough. Edgings for mats of a given size must be designed to fit them: a certain amount of easing is possible, and necessary round curves: but as the edging has usually a definite shape, and each repetition a definite size, this should not be unduly distorted. A mat must be made for the tatting rather than the tatting for the mat. This applies particularly to handkerchiefs, if these are prepared for exhibition.

Handkerchiefs

From what has already been said in the description of the two edgings (Figs. 88 and 89) it will be realized that the handkerchief presents several problems, especially if the repetition is a long one, and the rounds, if more than one, are dissimilar. To become familiar with edgings, make several very simple ones, for example, of rings alone, joined by spaces of thread instead of chains, which can be eased round corners and applied to squares of any size. Then consider making some with longer repetitions with special corner motifs, for which an exact measured square will be necessary.

For white handkerchiefs, fine linen or thin lawn is the best material. Handkerchiefs can be used as bought, but they should be absolutely plain: one row of hem-stitching at most, if at all. An ornamental weave may involve difficulties. If the edge is machined, cut if off: hand and machine work should not be combined. If the hem has been hand-rolled, which good linen handkerchiefs are, undo it, and iron out: the roll will probably be too thick, and must be put in again by hand. If making an elaborate edging, you may have to cut the square to size: in this case linen bought by the yard is more satisfactory.

Ideally the selected edging should be made first: whatever the number of rounds, the size of the handkerchief is controlled by the length of the longest repetition, in whichever round it is situated. If the corner motif is more than a single ring, the space it occupies must be taken into account. For absolute accuracy, pin out the completed edging, if necessary on squared paper: measure the distance of a side and cut the linen to fit, allowing of course for the rolled hem. This is to exhibition standard. Otherwise, and more easily, work one corner and complete repetition: measure this and calculate the length of the side required, not forgetting the extra fraction of a repetition to balance a corner. After cutting and hemming the linen, sew on the piece already worked, and continue round, sewing as you go, every few inches.

Small coloured silk handkerchiefs can be attractively decorated by a single motif (preferably worked in silk) in self or contrasting colour, sewn on to the surface near one corner, but the back will show the stitches, so choose a design which will not require too many threads behind it.

An applied motif may be used as an insertion on the linen square, buttonholing round the edge where the piece is cut out, but this weakens the fabric and it tends to pull out of shape when washed. The best effect is given by a white medallion laid on to a thin lawn square, which is semi-transparent: it has a less rigid look than a buttonholed circle.

Sheets and pillowcases

Edgings made for these must be made to fit as the material cannot be cut, but as the hem of a sheet is of considerable length, even a pattern of a fairly long repetition can be eased on to it if the measurements do not exactly coincide. In some degree this also applies to a pillowcase, although (if you work right round it) the four corners limit the amount of easing possible.

Edgings and borders are really a study in themselves, and if you specialize in these it is worth making up sample pieces and taking their measurements, so that you have a record of their repetitions and the length of side of material which they will need.

Any other decoration, apart from embroidered initials and monograms should be excluded from linens bordered with tatting. Its particular charm – pattern formed from softly curving lines – is not enhanced by embroidery stitches, cut-out work, or even drawn thread work, all of which compete with it and are a distraction. A narrow edge of tatting can be added to a richly embroidered article or garment, but then tatting is the accessory, where it is quite appropriate.

Mounting a flower piece

The technique of mounting a flower piece is described in *A New Look in Tatting*, the essentials of which are as follows:

1. The mount, which can be material or paper, must have a reasonably flat surface (i.e. not a deep pile, or corrugated).
2. It must be possible to sew through it.
3. When the motifs are sewn into place, the material must be stiffened by stretching it over and fastening it to a cardboard backing.
3. The colour of the mount will darken considerably under glass.

Mark on the mount the outline of the finished picture, and arrange the motifs within these boundary lines, to form a spray, growing plant, wreath, swag, or whatever you choose. Sew each into place with as few stitches as possible, with matching thread if the pieces are in colour. Where there are several ends of threads from one motif (as in multiple stalks) these may be drawn through the mount and fastened at the back with Scotch tape.

PREPARING WORK FOR EXHIBITION

Mats, handkerchiefs, collars, etc. are usually shown stretched and flat, but handkerchiefs may be folded to show the most possible trimming. They should be firmly sewn on to stiff paper, if necessary pasted over a firm cardboard. The paper, which is only the background, should be unobtrusive (never patterned) but of a suitable colour to show off the work – a rich blue, like a laundry blue, is good for white. The paper should extend for a short distance beyond the mat, one inch or less. In the gallery, work will be laid on a table, in a glass case, hung on the wall, or merely leant against it, in company with all the other exhibits: it is important that it should look its best in whatever position it is placed. Pieces submitted should be in a state that will not be damaged by undue handling, which they may very likely receive.

If you are submitting more than one piece, see that the colour of the background mounts do not clash, in case they are put near together. It is seldom that an exhibitor is completely satisfied with the way her work is presented, but not everything can be in the central glass case with a spotlight focused on it. Criticism of the arrangements is not good manners, except on the occasion when a fine piece of tatting appears in the group labelled 'crochet'. This, most unfortunately, does occur, all too often. Such a gross distortion of fact should be brought to the attention of the organizers. If the comparatively small company of tatters existing in Great Britain today can dispel the widespread illusion that tatting is 'a kind of crochet', their efforts towards restoring this ancient and beautiful art to its rightful place amongst lace-makers will not have been in vain.

The Glossary

NOTES ON THE GLOSSARY

Most crafts have a vocabulary of their own, however small, certain words being invested with a particular meaning for that craft. The meanings of words change over periods of time, but many crafts have retained their original vocabulary, remaining resistant to contemporary language. Knotting, whose language is precise and explicit, is one of these. How many of its terms tatting originally absorbed we do not know, but it is curious that, derived from knotting and lace-making as it is, so few of the original (and current) terms of either have survived. This is presumably due to the fact that in this age of mechanisation it is not a gainful trade, it earns nobody's living, and is done purely for pleasure by people who like it: on such its very continuance depends. Therefore, since it can be in anybody's hands, the words used must be current and familiar to everyone if the craft is to remain alive.

The language of tatting (in English) is still fluid, absorbing new words with the times, but this has the disadvantage that writers do not always use the same terms in the same sense. The appended glossary is an attempt to assign a particular meaning for certain words, and that meaning only. Judging by earlier English books, this lack of co-ordination has always existed. The word ring, for example, does not appear before this century, and until then had many synonyms: with some writers it still does. It may therefore be presumptuous to make clear-cut definitions even now. But for the student of design, who deals with arrangements of stitches ('formations') which are quite definite in construction, it is essential that they should be defined: in which case they may conceivably bear a specific name to distinguish them. This would be an undoubted advantage to designers and workers alike both now and in the future.

In the glossary two words – scallop and vandyke – which do not have an exclusive meaning for tatting, have been included. They are not formations of stitches but an outline of a certain shape which can be produced in any medium. Since, however, tatting is frequently used to indicate both these specific outlines, their definitions have been given.

GLOSSARY OF TERMS USED IN TATTING

CHAIN — A row of tatted stitches worked on an independent thread, which therefore need not be drawn into a closed circle. An old name for the chain was 'a straight thread'.

CLOVER — The traditional name for a group of three rings, the centre one either larger or smaller than those at the sides. Usually joined to one another.

DAISY — The traditional name for a motif consisting of a central ring surrounded by (usually eight) rings which are worked on the same thread.

DOUBLE STITCH — The complete tatting stitch, composed of two half-hitches, a right and a left turn, to form an inverted lark's head.

EYELET — The tatted ring in seamanship.

FALSE CHAIN — A suggested name for an early form of the chain, in which the stitches (unturned) are formed by the shuttle thread on an impassive running line, of fixed length.

FRIVOLITÉ — The French, and now internationally used name for tatting.

HALF-RING — A suggested name for a tatted ring not completely drawn up, leaving part of the thread unworked. (Has also been described as a scallop, which shape it resembles.)

JOSEPHINE RING — A small tatted ring made of half-stitches all of one kind: also called the Josephine knot: originally described as the Josephine picot.

KNOTTING — A row of 'knots', lying closely together on the thread which forms them: each knot consisting of three turns on a loop.

LINK-PICOT — A suggested name for a very small picot, used for joining.

LOCKING STITCH — A suggested name for a stitch not turned, therefore locking the passage of the running thread.

MEDALLION — Originally meant 'A large medal of antique character'. In needlework and tatting the term is extended to describe an arrangement of lines which make up a complete design, the outline usually circular or square.

MOCK-RING	A suggested name for a chain with the end brought round to a point at or near the beginning, giving the effect of a ring.
MOTIF	The theme or dominant element in a composition. Used in both abstract and concrete sense.
PEARL AND RAISED TATTING	The result of the introduction of one or more threads held in the left hand, the shuttle working on them alternately, thus producing picots or 'pearls' spontaneously. (Now obsolete.)
PICOT	A protruding loop of thread formed between two double stitches, for the purpose of ornament or joining. Originally called a 'pearl', or 'purl'.
REPETITION	A fraction of a pattern which is exactly repeated for the required number of times to form the whole.
RING	A loop of thread entirely covered with tatted stitches, and drawn into a closed circle. Old names for the ring are: oval, lozenge, rosette, and loop. A very small ring was a dot, or oeillet.
RUNNING LINE	The thread upon which the stitches are carried.
SCALLOP	An ornamental edging in any medium, of small semi-circular lobes, in imitation of the shell of the scallop, a bivalve mollusc.
SCROLL	A suggested name for a series of rings, connected by chains: or rings carried at intervals on one long chain.
SPACE (of thread)	The length of thread between one ring and the next. Also between one double stitch and the next, in which case it becomes a picot when drawn up.
TATTING	A kind of knotted lace, made on the hand, the thread carried upon a shuttle.
VANDYKE	Each of a series of large points forming a border to lace, cloth, etc. Common in portraits by the Flemish painter Van Dyck.
WHEEL	The traditional name for a central ring, surrounded by a row of rings carried on both sides of a line. The inner rings of the row are attached to the centre.

Bibliography

KNOTS, USEFUL AND ORNAMENTAL. George Russell Shaw, Cambridge (Mass.), U.S.A.
LEARN TO TAT. J. & P. Coats Ltd., Paisley.
TATTING, Book 1. Penelope, Manchester.
LA FRIVOLITÉ. Thérèse de Dillmont, Bibliothèque D.M.C., France.
ENCYCLOPAEDIA OF NEEDLEWORK. Thérèse de Dillmont, Alsace.
TATTING ILLUSTRATED. Norma Benporath, Melbourne, Australia.
SCHIFFCHENARBEIT. Wiesbaden, Germany.
IL LAVORO CHIACCHIERINO. Milan, Italy.
FRIVOLITETSMÖNSTER. Sara Lawergren, Malmö, Sweden.
PRIMORES FEMENINOS. Barcelona, Spain.
THE ART OF TATTING. Lady Hoare, London.
THE ILLUSTRATED EXHIBITOR AND MAGAZINE OF ART. London.
A NEW LOOK IN TATTING. E. A. Nicholls, London.
Books by Mlle Eleonore Riego de la Branchardière:
The Tatting Book, 1850, and subsequent editions.
Tatting Edgings and Insertions, 1861.
Golden Stars in Tatting and Crochet, 1861.
The Exhibition Tatting Book, 1862.
The Complete Tatting Book, 1863 and 1866.
The Royal Tatting Book, 1864.
The Lace Tatting Book, 1866.
Simple Book of Tatting, 1867.
The Pearl Tatting Book, 1867.
The Raised Tatting Book, 1868.
TATTING MADE EASY, 1851. 'A lady', London.
THE LADIES' HANDBOOK OF MILLINERY, DRESSMAKING AND TATTING, 1843.
THE LADIES' WORKTABLE BOOK, 1850.
BEETON'S BOOK OF NEEDLEWORK, 1870.
DICTIONARY OF NEEDLEWORK. Caulfeild and Saward.
Periodicals, from 1860:
The Englishwoman's Domestic Magazine: an illustrated journal, combining practical information, instruction and amusement.
The Young Englishwoman: a volume of pure literature, new fashions and pretty needlework designs.

Index

INDEX